CAMBRIDGE
UNIVERSITY PRESS

CAMBRIDGE ENGLISH
Language Assessment
Part of the University of Cambridge

Cambridge English
Compact
Key for Schools

Workbook without answers

Frances Treloar

CAMBRIDGE
UNIVERSITY PRESS

University Printing House, Cambridge CB2 8BS, United Kingdom

One Liberty Plaza, 20th Floor, New York, NY 10006, USA

477 Williamstown Road, Port Melbourne, VIC 3207, Australia

4843/24, 2nd Floor, Ansari Road, Daryaganj, Delhi – 110002, India

79 Anson Road, #06–04/06, Singapore 079906

Cambridge University Press is part of the University of Cambridge.

It furthers the University's mission by disseminating knowledge in the pursuit of education, learning and research at the highest international levels of excellence.

www.cambridge.org
Information on this title: www.cambridge.org/9781107618800

First published 2014
20 19 18 17 16 15 14 13 12 11 10

Printed in Spain by GraphyCems

A catalogue record for this publication is available from the British Library

ISBN 978-1-107-61863-3 Student's Book without answers with CD-ROM
ISBN 978-1-107-61880-0 Workbook without answers with Audio CD
ISBN 978-1-107-61872-5 Teacher's Book
ISBN 978-1-107-61868-8 Class Audio CD
ISBN 978-1-107-61874-9 Presentation Plus
ISBN 978-1-107-61879-4 Student's Pack (Student's Book without answers with CD-ROM, Workbook without answers with Audio CD)

Additional resources for this publication at www.cambridge.org/compactkeyforschools

CONTENTS

Grammar

have got

1 Write sentences or questions with the correct form of *have got*.

1 John and Jo / black hair
John and Jo have got black hair.
2 John and Jo / blue eyes?
Have John and Jo got blue eyes?
3 We / six cousins
....
4 you / sisters?
....
5 She / not / brothers
....
6 Harry / very short fair hair
....
7 Molly / a nickname?
....
8 We / not / our trainers
....

2 Exam candidates often make mistakes with *have got*. Correct the mistakes in these sentences.

1 I ~~got~~ a new school bag for sale. have got
2 In my house, I get a present for you.
3 It's a very good camera because it had got two screens.
4 The old TV has got three years old.
5 There has got lots of shops, museums and beautiful beaches.
6 The handbag has got black colour.
7 Sorry, but I'm a lot of exams and I cannot go to the cinema with you.
8 Have you got an age between twenty and twenty-seven years old?

Present simple

3 Read the information about Ryan and complete the sentences.

	On school days	In the holidays
wake up	6.50	9.45
walk to school	8.25	
have lunch	12.20	1.00
do homework	6.30	
watch TV	7.00	10.00, 2.00, 8.00
go to bed	9.15	10.30

1 Ryan ....wakes up..... at ten to seven on school days.
2 He .... at twenty-five past eight on school days, but he .... in the holidays.
3 He .... at one o'clock in the holidays.
4 He .... his homework at 6.30 on school days, but he .... any homework in the holidays.
5 He .... TV a lot in the holidays.
6 He .... at quarter past nine on school days.

Question words

4 Complete the questions with these words. Use each word once.

~~What time~~ When How Where What Who

1 What time do you get up on school days?
2 .... does your dad travel to work?
3 .... do you have for breakfast?
4 .... is your school?
5 .... is your best friend?
6 .... do your friends come to your house?

5 Answer the questions in Exercise 4 for you. Write complete sentences.

1 I get up at half past seven on school days.

Vocabulary

1 **Complete Joanna's sentences with these words, then find the people in the picture.**

~~sisters~~ grandmother uncle grandparents husband daughter cousins

1 I've got one brother but I haven't got any ..*sisters*.. .
2 I am my parents' only ....
3 My aunt Diana is married to my .... Jacob.
4 Diana and Jacob have got two sons, Ben and Joe. Ben and Joe are my favourite ....
5 My aunt Katie hasn't got a .... – she doesn't want to get married yet.
6 My .... (my mum's mother and father) are both 65 years old.
7 My grandfather is one month younger than my ....

2 **1 Listen and check your answers.**

3 **Match the sentence halves.**

1 Daisy has got a pair of trainers
2 Freddie has got some pencils
3 Daisy has got a diary
4 Freddie has got a mobile
5 Daisy has got some money
6 Freddie has got a snack
7 Daisy has got a towel

a for a swimming lesson.
b in a blue purse.
c to wear for a basketball lesson.
d to write homework in.
e to call mum at lunchtime.
f for drawing pictures.
g because teenagers are always hungry!

4 **2 Listen and check your answers.**

5 **Match the items with the correct bag. Use Exercise 3 to help you. There are two extra items you don't need.**

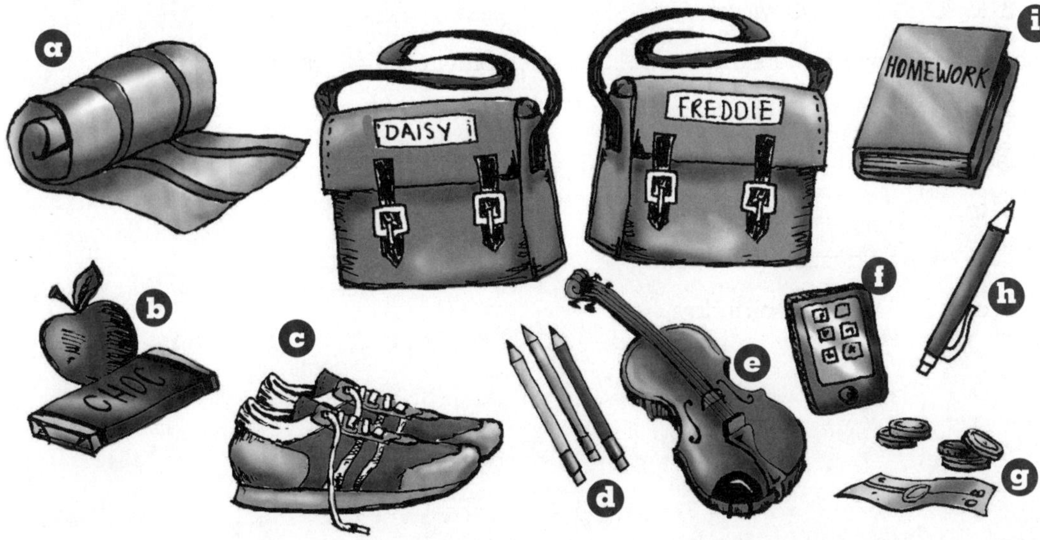

Exam tasks

Reading Part 2

Read the sentences about Zara's family.

Choose the best word (A, B or C) for each space.

0 I'm Zara and my big family is .... unusual.

A often **B** too **C** quite

1 My brothers' names all start with the .... 'B': Bradley, Bernie and Bennie.

A surname **B** word **C** letter

2 My brothers all .... the same, too.

A see **B** look **C** watch

3 When they are not together, my brothers always .... each other on their mobiles.

A talk **B** send **C** text

4 My brothers and I have all got .... red hair.

A straight **B** true **C** right

5 I am the same .... as my oldest brother's son!

A year **B** age **C** birthday

Writing Part 6

Read the descriptions of some words from Unit 1.

What is the word for each one?

The first letter is already there. There is one space for each other letter in the word.

0	This is something that young children and babies play with.	t o y
1	You wear these on your feet when you do sports.	t _ _ _ _ _ _ _
2	These are two brothers or sisters who are born on the same day.	t _ _ _ _
3	People usually put this instrument on their shoulder to play it.	v _ _ _ _ _
4	You eat this meal in the evening.	d _ _ _ _ _
5	These are part of your face and you see with them.	e _ _ _

Listening Part 3

3 Listen to Kelly talking to her mum about her violin lessons.

For each question, choose the right answer (A, B or C).

0 This week, Kelly's violin teacher is

A ill.
(**B**) on a course.
C doing an exam.

1 When is Kelly's next violin lesson?

A 8th August
B 15th August
C 22nd August

2 Where will they get the music book?

A the bookshop
B the library
C the music shop

3 Which day will they get the book?

A Tuesday
B Wednesday
C Thursday

4 Kelly's mum will pick Kelly up at

A 3.45 p.m.
B 4.00 p.m.
C 4.15 p.m.

5 What kind of food will they eat afterwards?

A pizza
B fish
C burgers

2 In my free time

Grammar

Adverbs of frequency

1 Write sentences about Danny's week. Use these words and phrases.

twice a week | every day except Sunday | often | ~~once a week~~ | on Sundays | never

Monday:	Go to school in Dad's car, piano lesson 5.15 p.m., band practice 6.00 p.m.
Tuesday:	Go to school in Dad's car, band practice 6.00 p.m.
Wednesday:	Walk to school, swimming club after school, band practice 5.30 p.m.
Thursday:	Go to school in Dad's car, band practice 5.00 p.m.
Friday:	Walk to school, band practice 4.00 p.m.
Saturday:	Swimming club 10.00 a.m., band practice 6.00 p.m.
Sunday:	Visit Grandpa as usual!

1 have / a piano lesson — Danny has a piano lesson once a week.
2 have / band practice ....
3 go / to school in his dad's car ....
4 visit / his grandfather ....
5 have / swimming club ....
6 go / to stamp club ....

2 Exam candidates often make mistakes with the order of sentences which describe frequency. Correct the mistakes in these sentences.

1 You know ~~always I like~~ make-up. I always like
2 I every day played table tennis.
3 The weather was beautiful always there.
4 Always I watch the competition with my father and sister.
5 I can usually once a week write.
6 The weather sometimes was good and hot but sometimes it rained.

Do you like …? / Would you like …?

3 Complete the conversation with the correct form of *would like, like* or *don't like.*

Julian: Did you go to Music Club yesterday?
Peter: No, they played jazz and I (1) don't like jazz much.
Julian: What kind of music (2) ....?
Peter: Rock, pop, classical – most kinds, but not jazz!
Julian: I (3) .... to come too. Can I just come or do I have to ask the teacher first?
Peter: Just come when you want to. (4) .... to come with me next week?
Julian: Yes, please. I (5) .... to join so I can learn to play an instrument.
Peter: (6) .... all kinds of music?
Julian: I (7) .... modern music best, but I (8) .... to learn more about classical and jazz, too.
Peter: Music Club will be perfect for you!

4 4 Listen and check your answers.

Vocabulary

1 Write the name of the clubs.

~~cinema~~ camping art camera tennis music stamp

Which club do they go to?

1 Harry likes watching films. ...cinema... club
2 Greg loves sleeping in a tent and eating outside. .... club
3 Natalia likes doing sports with her friends. .... club
4 Celia likes taking photographs. .... club
5 Terry enjoys playing the guitar and singing. .... club
6 Sarah likes collecting things. .... club
7 Jack enjoys drawing and painting pictures. .... club

2 Write the names of the people in the picture in Exercise 1.

3 Complete the sentences with the **opposite** words in the box.

~~hates~~ interested in prefers loves enjoy terrible at doesn't like

1 Ellie loves watching films. Maisie ...hates.... watching films.
2 Ellie hates cooking. Maisie .... cooking.
3 Ellie enjoys singing. Maisie .... singing.
4 Ellie likes going to concerts. Maisie doesn't .... going to concerts.
5 Ellie is very good at playing computer games. Maisie is .... playing computer games.
6 Ellie likes dancing more than doing sports. Maisie .... doing sports to dancing.
7 Ellie thinks history is boring. Maisie is .... history.

4 5 Listen and check your answers.

5 Complete the sentences for you. Use the correct form of words from Exercise 3.

1 I .... cooking.
2 I .... singing.
3 I'm .... at dancing.
4 I'm .... in science.
5 I .... playing computer games.
6 I .... going to the cinema.

Exam tasks

Reading Part 3a

Complete the five conversations.

Circle **A**, **B** or **C**.

0

How old are you?

(A) Fourteen.

B Fine thanks.

C How do you do?

1	Do you like sharing a bedroom with your sister?	**A**	I'd love to.
		B	It's usually OK.
		C	We've got purple walls!
2	When can we practise together for the concert?	**A**	All right, what time?
		B	For an hour and half.
		C	Are you busy on Thursday?
3	We'd like some chips with our burgers, please.	**A**	Really? I don't.
		B	Are they large ones?
		C	And some salad?
4	Are you coming to Tennis Club with us on Friday?	**A**	What a pity!
		B	I'm afraid not.
		C	Not bad, thank you.
5	Let's go swimming as soon as we get to the lake.	**A**	Great idea!
		B	How about the beach?
		C	There you are.

Listening Part 4

1 6 Listen and tick (✔) the answers you hear.

1	Tuesday	☐	Thursday	✔
2	Saturdays	☐	Sundays	☐
3	Caponacre	☐	Caponekar	☐
4	Camilla	☐	Cammile	☐
5	7.15 p.m.	☐	6.45 p.m.	☐
6	£3.50	☐	$3.50	☐

2 7 You will hear a girl, Becky, telling her friend, Milo, about a cookery club.

Listen and complete each question.

Cookery Club

Day:	Friday
Number of club members:	**(1)** ....
This week:	Learn to make **(2)** ....
Next week's teacher:	Miss **(3)** ....
Time:	**(4)** .... p.m.
Cost this week:	**(5)** £............................

Writing Part 7

Complete these emails.

Write ONE word for each space.

From: Frederica
To: Marie

Hi Marie,

Can you help **(0)** .....me.....? I want **(1)** .... make a birthday card for my grandma. I know you're very good **(2)** .... art, so **(3)** .... you got any ideas? Grandma loves animals. She has three cats, two dogs **(4)** .... two horses. **(5)** .... you think I should paint one **(6)** .... her animals for the card?

Frederica

From: Marie
To: Frederica

Hi Frederica,

It **(7)** .... difficult to paint animals well. But you can **(8)** .... a photo of her pets with my brilliant new camera. **(9)** .... you like to borrow it? Then we can make a card with the photo on the computer. I think that will look better **(10)** .... a painting. I'll ring you later.

Marie

3 Eating in, eating out

Grammar

There is / are, a / an, some & any

1 Choose the correct two words in each sentence.

1. There *is / are a / some* chicken in the garden!
2. *Are / Is* there *a / any* chairs in the kitchen?
3. There *is / are any / some* orange juice for you in the fridge.
4. Why *is / are* there *a / an* fish on the table?
5. There *aren't / isn't a / any* clock in the hall.
6. There *aren't / isn't some / any* rice in the cupboard.
7. Do you think there *is / are any / a* vegetables in this soup?

How much / many? a lot, a little, a few

2 Write the questions.

1. apples in the bowl
   How many apples are there in the bowl?
2. milk in the fridge
   ....
3. flowers in the garden
   ....
4. pictures in the hall
   ....
5. meat on the plate
   ....
6. potatoes in the bag
   ....
7. jam on the bread
   ....

3 Look at the pictures and write answers for the questions in Exercise 2.

1. There are a few apples in the bowl.
2. ....
3. ....
4. ....
5. ....
6. ....
7. ....

4 8 Listen and check your answers.

(don't) have to

5 Read the information about a brother and sister's jobs for the week. Complete the sentences with the correct form of *have to*.

Job	Samantha	Adam
wash the dishes	✘	✔
tidy the living room	✔	✘
make his / her bed	✔	✔
wash the kitchen floor	✔	✘
tidy his / her bedroom	✔	✔
clean the bathroom	✘	✔

1. Samantha ...doesn't have to wash. the dishes this week.
2. Adam ...has to wash............. the dishes this week.
3. Samantha .... the living room this week.
4. Adam .... the living room this week.
5. Adam and Samantha both .... their bedrooms this week.
6. Samantha .... the kitchen floor this week.
7. Adam and Samantha both .... their beds this week.
8. Adam .... the kitchen floor this week.
9. Samantha .... the bathroom this week.
10. Adam .... the bathroom this week.

Vocabulary

1 Find ten furniture words. Tick (✔) the correct picture when you find a word.

S	O	F	A	C	H	L	O	P
F	D	O	C	O	L	F	M	B
C	U	P	B	O	A	R	D	E
H	W	A	E	K	M	I	E	M
A	D	E	A	E	P	D	S	O
I	C	H	M	R	M	G	K	F
R	S	S	H	O	W	E	R	A
T	T	O	I	L	E	T	J	U
H	O	F	M	I	R	R	O	R

2 Write the names of the rooms.

1 There's a whiteboard on the wall and there are lots of desks. ......classroom........
2 There's a shower and a toilet with a sink next to it. ....
3 There's a TV on the wall, a sofa, a low table and a tall lamp on the floor. ....
4 Between the two beds, there's a cupboard with a clock on it. ....
5 There are lots of cupboards, a fridge and a cooker. ....
6 People go into this small room when they come into the house. There is a large mirror on the wall. ....

3 The information in these sentences is wrong. Correct the endings.

1 An omelette is made from ~~bread~~. ....eggs.........
2 Rice is usually red or blue. ....
3 People usually make soup with meat or fruit. ....
4 Juice is nice to eat. ....
5 Salad is usually hot. ....
6 Chickens are a kind of plant. ....
7 Fish live in trees or flowers. ....
8 Onions are square. ....

4 9 Listen and check your answers.

Exam tasks

Reading Part 5

Read the article about a girl who lives in Japan.

Choose the best word (**A**, **B**, or **C**) for each space.

My life

My name's Akiyoshi. I'm thirteen **(0)** .... I live in Osaka, a Japanese city. I'm going to tell you **(1)** .... a day in my life.

Every morning I eat breakfast at a low table which **(2)** .... called a 'kotatsu'. When I walk to school, I **(3)** .... to wear a red hat and jacket. We go to school Monday to Friday and sometimes **(4)** .... Saturday mornings, too. Our school subjects **(5)** .... art, music, maths and Japanese. I think Japanese is harder to write **(6)** .... any other language.

We eat lunch in the classroom **(7)** .... our teacher. Then we clean the classroom and halls. We pick up paper and clean the desks. We clean everything!

When I get home, the first thing I do is take off my shoes. I eat supper, watch a **(8)** .... TV shows, do my homework and go to bed.

0	(**A**) and	**B** so	**C** but
1	**A** for	**B** about	**C** over
2	**A** be	**B** is	**C** are
3	**A** must	**B** can	**C** have
4	**A** in	**B** at	**C** on
5	**A** include	**B** includes	**C** including
6	**A** like	**B** as	**C** than
7	**A** with	**B** from	**C** into
8	**A** few	**B** little	**C** lot

Listening Part 5

10 You will hear a woman on the TV talking about a new programme for teenagers. Listen and complete each question.

New TV programme

Name:	Hot Food
First programme is about:	**(1)** ....
Place programmes filmed in:	**(2)** ....
Number to call with ideas:	**(3)** ....
Day of the week:	**(4)** ....
Start time:	**(5)** .... p.m.

Writing Part 8

Read the advertisement and the email.

Fill in the information in Tom's notes.

Riverside Farm

Fun activities every day:

11.00 a.m. Make cheese

2. 00 p.m. See the animals

3. 00 p.m. Ride motorbikes around farm

£6.75 per person or £8.50 including café meal

From: Mr Taylor

To: Tom Tyson

School Farm Trip

Our coach goes to the farm from school at 10.30 a.m. and returns at 5.00 p.m. After the morning activity, we'll have lunch in the café (so we'll pay the higher price per person) and stay at the farm until 4.00 p.m. You don't have to wear school uniform but please bring a raincoat.

Tom's notes

Farm trip

Name of farm:	Riverside
Leave school at:	1 a.m.
What to take:	2
Travel to farm by:	3
Morning activity:	4
Cost:	5 £

4 What are you doing now?

Grammar

Present continuous

1 Complete Sarah and Molly's messages with the correct form of the present continuous.

Where are you, Molly?
11.03

I (1) 'm sitting (sit) on the train to Markham with my mum.
11.05

Oh, (2) .... (you / go) shopping?
11.07

No, we (3) .... (not go) shopping. We (4) .... (go) to Markham to help my aunt. She (5) .... (move) into a new house today. What (6) .... (you / do) ?
11.08

I (7) .... (wait) for a bus. I (8) .... (go) shopping in Markham!
11.10

2 Write sentences about the picture. Use the correct present continuous form of the verbs in brackets.

1 (listen) He's listening to music.
2 (fish) ....
3 (drink) ....
4 (wear) ....
5 (sit) ....
6 (eat) ....
7 (read) ....

Present simple vs present continuous

3 Complete the sentences with the correct form of the verbs in brackets.

1 Simon ....likes........ (like) skateboarding.
2 I usually .... (practise) with my basketball team on Saturday afternoons.
3 What .... Mark .... (do) this morning? Can he come with us to the swimming pool?
4 Dave .... (not want) to go to hockey club again.
5 I can't speak to you at the moment because I .... (play) football.
6 Jane and Helen .... (play) tennis on Tuesdays.
7 I .... (not do) any sport this week because I've got a bad leg.
8 When .... Leona .... (have) her badminton lessons?
9 Dear Harry, How are you? I .... (write) this email to tell you about yesterday's match.

Vocabulary

1 Complete the words with *ing*, *ball* or *boarding*.

1	ski...ing...	f
2	swimm.........	
3	basket.........	
4	snow..........	
5	volley..........	
6	cycl.........	
7	ice-skat.........	
8	surf.........	
9	skate..........	
10	foot.........	

2 Match the words in Exercise 1 with the correct object.

3 Put the letters in the correct order to make sports.

1	stnien	..tennis.	b
2	lofg	....	
3	ceokhy	....	
4	alebt esntni	....	
5	ialettcsh	....	
6	lratmai rast	....	
7	soerbica	....	

4 Match the words in Exercise 3 with the correct object.

5 Complete the sentences with these words.

~~play~~	lose	do	throw	train	go

1 Do you ...play... volleyball in a team?
2 I'd like to .... cycling when we're on holiday.
3 Janey and Maria .... aerobics every Monday evening.
4 You must .... the ball over the net.
5 How often do you .... for the competition with your coach?
6 I won't be happy if we .... the match.

6 11 Listen and check your answers.

7 Where do you wear these clothes? Write the correct letter or letters.

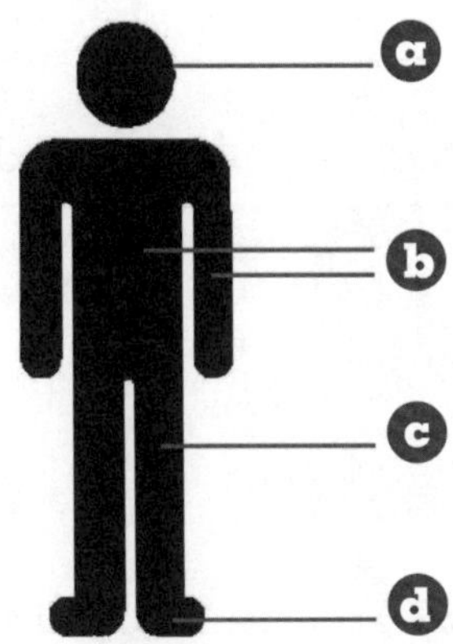

T-shirt ......b.....	trainers	hat ....
socks c and d	jeans	shirt ....
skirt	boots	sweater ....
trousers	shorts	dress ....
jacket	coat	

Exam tasks

Listening Part 1

12 You will hear five short conversations.

There is one question for each conversation.

For each question, choose the right answer (**A**, **B** or **C**).

1 Where is Jessie playing table tennis?

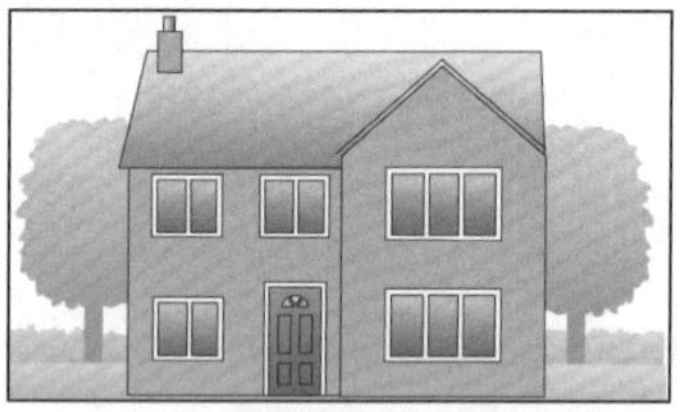

A

B

C

2 What does the girl's football team wear?

A

B

C

3 What time is Henry's skiing lesson?

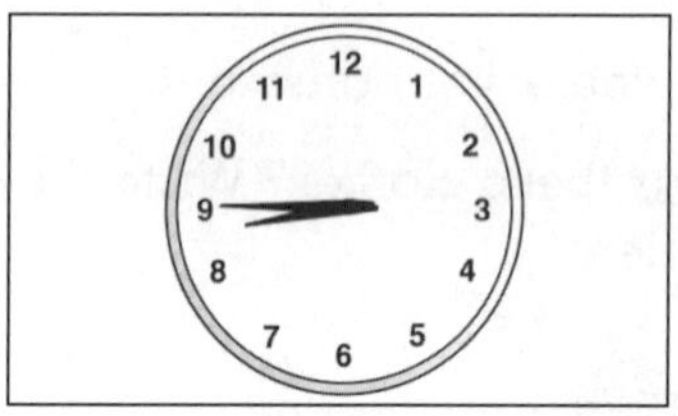

A

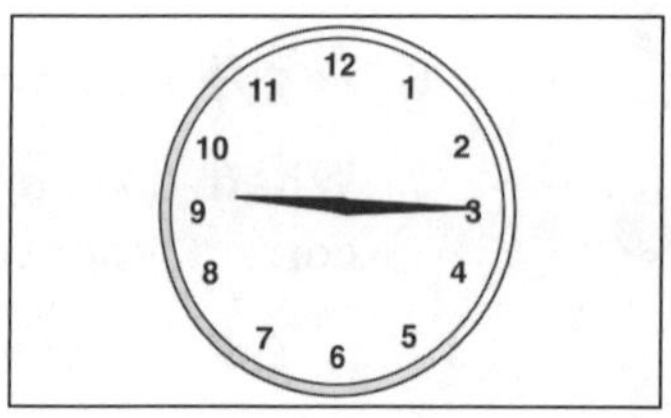

B

C

4 What is Mum's aerobics teacher doing this evening?

A

B

C

5 Where did Liz sell her football ticket?

A

B

C

Reading Part 4

Read the article about football match tickets.

Are sentences **1–7** 'Right' **(A)** or 'Wrong' **(B)**?

If there is not enough information to answer 'Right' **(A)** or 'Wrong' **(B)**, choose 'Doesn't say' **(C)**.

The Price of Football

My name is Ashley Parkes. Nine months ago, I started playing football for my school. The team coach told us to go and see as many football matches as possible to help us play better. I decided to go and see one of the big, famous football clubs play a match. My mum and dad wanted to come with me, and they agreed to pay for the tickets. When Mum asked me how much football tickets were, I couldn't answer, so I went online to find out. What a nasty surprise! The cheapest tickets for the next match were £41($65, €44) – £123 for the three of us. There weren't any discounts for children or students. And a ticket for the whole football year cost £999 per person!

I told Mum the match ticket price, and she said it was too much. Then Dad said, 'Why don't we go and watch our town club on Saturday? It's a small club, but they're playing well at the moment and I don't think it'll cost £41 each to see them!' On their website, I found some tickets for the match. They cost £15 for adults with a seat, or £13 standing up, but under-16s only pay £6 with or without a seat. What a difference! We went to the match and enjoyed it so much that we joined the club and now we go to every game.

0 Ashley has played football in the school team for several years.
A Right (**B**) Wrong **C** Doesn't say

1 The football coach took the team to watch some matches.
A Right **B** Wrong **C** Doesn't say

2 Ashley knew how expensive the big football club's tickets were before he went online.
A Right **B** Wrong **C** Doesn't say

3 The lowest price for a ticket to the big club's match was £41.
A Right **B** Wrong **C** Doesn't say

4 Match tickets for the big club cost less for young people.
A Right **B** Wrong **C** Doesn't say

5 Ashley's dad has been to see the small club play many times before.
A Right **B** Wrong **C** Doesn't say

6 A 15-year-old's ticket cost £15 for sitting and watching the small club's match.
A Right **B** Wrong **C** Doesn't say

7 Ashley is now a member of his town's football club.
A Right **B** Wrong **C** Doesn't say

Writing Part 9

Read the email from your English friend, Ali.

Write an email to Ali and answer the questions.

Write 25–35 words.

From: Ali
To: Tom Tyson

We've got a new sports centre in our town and I play volleyball there. Where is your nearest sports centre? Which sports are played there? How often do you do sports there?

5 Great places to visit

Grammar

Past simple

1 Write the past simple forms.

1 study	studied	**4** enjoy	....	**6** find	....
2 drink	....	**5** try	....	**7** open	....
3 eat	....				

2 Complete the text with the correct form of the past simple.

Last summer, Simon **(1)** ....went.... (go) with his family to camp in a tent near a castle in the mountains. It **(2)** .... (be) a beautiful place but as soon as they arrived it **(3)** .... (start) to rain and it **(4)** .... (not stop) for four days! During the day, they **(5)** .... (not do) any activities because it was too wet outside and at night, they **(6)** .... (not sleep) because the wind and the rain **(7)** .... (be) so noisy. On the fifth day, the man who lived in the castle **(8)** .... (invite) them to stay inside the castle! After that, Simon and his family **(9)** .... (have) a great time. They **(10)** .... (not mind) the bad weather because they **(11)** .... (play) games in the castle all day and they **(12)** .... (not hear) the rain and the wind at night.

3 13 Listen and check your answers.

4 Write the questions, then write true answers.

1 time / go to bed last night?
What time did you go to bed last night?
I went to bed at half past nine.

2 when / you / born?
....

3 what time / get up / this morning?
....

4 where / you / go / last weekend?
....

5 what / you / have / for breakfast today?
....

Time expressions: *in* / *at* / *on*; *ago*

5 Complete the sentences with *ago*, *in*, *at* or *on*.

1 I only bought this jacket two weeks .... and it looks old already!
2 Grandma's train left .... nine o'clock this morning.
3 I didn't go to school .... Wednesday because I had a bad tooth.
4 It was really hot .... August.
5 My sister got married .... 15th July.
6 My grandfather was born .... 1946.

Vocabulary

1 Match the sentences with the words.

1 People go to this place to see concerts or sports matches.
2 This place is very old and was built to keep the people who lived in it safe.
3 People go to this place to study or to borrow books to read at home.
4 Things like cars, toys and TVs are made in this place.
5 You go here to see plays.
6 You go here to see things from other centuries and other countries.

a a factory
b a castle
c a library
d a stadium
e a museum
f a theatre

2 Match the pictures with the places in Exercise 1.

3 Complete the sentences with these words. There is one extra place.

~~library~~ bookshop newsagent supermarket police station department store bank

1 I took my books back to the ...library... this morning.
2 We went shopping in the big .... on Grace Street so we could get all our food for the week.
3 There's a .... at the end of our street that sells newspapers and magazines and nothing else.
4 We went to the new .... on Saturday because I wanted a new dress and my mum wanted to buy some make-up.
5 My mum is a .... manager so she knows a lot about borrowing and saving money.
6 I sometimes go to a .... when I want to buy something to read.

4 Write the dates. Find out what happened on these dates.

1 the twenty-second of November, nineteen sixty-three — 22/11/1963 – President John F Kennedy was killed.

2 the third of August, fourteen ninety-two ....

3 the tenth of March, eighteen seventy-six ....

4 the fourth of July, seventeen seventy-six ....

5 the seventeenth of December, nineteen oh three ....

6 the twentieth of July, nineteen sixty-nine ....

Exam tasks

Reading Part 2

Read the sentences about going shopping.

Choose the best word (**A**, **B** or **C**) for each space.

0 Yesterday, my older brother and I .... shopping in the city centre.

A had (**B**) went **C** took

1 We wanted to .... a present for our dad's birthday.

A get **B** bring **C** look

2 We didn't have a lot of money to .... on the present.

A use **B** put **C** spend

3 We found a great book for Dad in a shop but it .... too much.

A cost **B** paid **C** earned

4 We looked on the internet and found the same book on a cheap ....

A computer **B** website **C** screen

5 The book we found online was .... than the one in the shop so we bought it.

A lower **B** worse **C** cheaper

Listening Part 5

1 14 You will hear some information about a museum. Listen and complete each question.

<u>Museum of Pop Music</u>

Address:	Victoria Square
Name of this month's exhibition:	(1) ....
Date exhibition ends:	(2) ....
Fashion room:	(3) pop stars' ....
Cheap travel by:	(4) ....
Price for teenagers:	(5) £..............................

2 Write questions and answers about the museum in Exercise 1.

1 address?
....

2 name / exhibition?
....

3 when / exhibition end?
....

4 what / in new fashion room?
....

5 cheap travel tickets?
....

6 cost for teenagers?
....

Writing Part 9

Yesterday you bought a music CD.

Write an email to your English friend, Sam.

Say:

- **what** CD you bought
- **where** you bought the CD
- **why** you like the CD.

Write 25–35 words.

6 Getting there

Grammar

Comparative and superlative adjectives

1 **Complete the sentences with the comparative form of the adjectives in brackets.**

1 Cars are .... (big) than motorbikes.
2 Planes are .... (expensive) than buses.
3 Ships are .... (slow) than planes.
4 Motorbikes are .... (small) than lorries.
5 City roads are .... (busy) than country roads.
6 Trains are .... (fast) than bicycles.

2 **Exam candidates often make mistakes with superlative adjectives. Correct one mistake in each of these sentences.**

1 I think it is the ~~older~~ car in the village. My grandfather bought it in 1955. oldest
2 You can go to Oto by train which is the most easy way.
3 We can go by bus, which is the most cheapest way.
4 I'm going to use a pink colour to paint my bedroom. I'll start at 9.00 a.m. You should wear your most old clothes.
5 This competition was one of the beast competitions I've ever seen.
6 I will take you to the most big shopping centre to buy what you need.
7 In my home town the best interesting place is the 'Ya lu jiang' River.
8 I went to Ho Chi Minh City. It is one of the bigest cities in my country.

3 **Look at the chart. Write sentences using the correct form of the words and phrases in brackets.**

	World Train Journeys		
	A The Orient Express, Paris to Istanbul	B Pride of Africa, Cape Town to Dar es Salaam	C Deccan Odyssey, Delhi to Mumbai
Journey time	1 week	2 weeks	8 days
Journey distance	3,186 km	1,600 km	1,161 km
Ticket price	$19,900	$14,900	$6,650
Date of first train	1883	1989	2004

Time
1 (long – comparative) Journey C ....is longer than journey A.......
2 (short – superlative) Journey ....A is the shortest......................

Distance
3 (far – comparative) Journey B ....
4 (long – superlative) Journey ....

Price
5 (cheap – comparative) Journey B ....
6 (expensive – superlative) Journey ....

Age
7 (old – comparative) Train B ....
8 (new – superlative) Train ....

4 15 Listen and check your answers.

Vocabulary

1 Look at the key. Write the correct letters next to each form of transport.

Key
A two wheels
B four or more wheels
C usually goes on roads
D flies
E goes on water
F carries more than ten people

1 plane A, D, F
2 lorry ....
3 bicycle ....
4 ship ....
5 car ....
6 bus ....
7 boat ....
8 train ....
9 tram ....
10 motorbike ....

2 **Complete the sentences with the correct verb, then answer the questions.**

~~travel~~ sail drive ride walk fly

1 How do you usually ..travel.. when you go on holiday?
2 Do most students .... to your school or do they go by bus or car?
3 Which airport do people in your town .... from?
4 Can ten-year-olds .... cars in your country?
5 Does anyone in your family .... a motorbike?
6 How long does it take for a ship to .... around the world?

3 16 **Listen and check your answers. What were the girl's answers?**

4 Look at the map. Complete the directions with these phrases.

~~along~~ in front of your left Festival Bridge turn right turn left

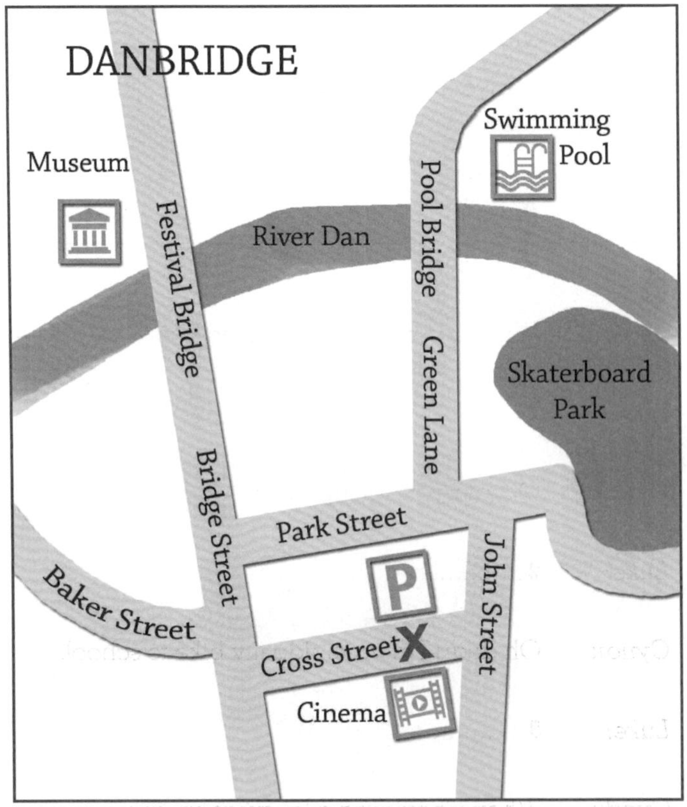

You have just come out of Cross Street car park and you are looking at the cinema. How do you get to ...?

The museum
Walk (1) ...along... Cross Street to Bridge Street and (2) .... Walk down to the river and go across (3) .... The museum is on (4) ....

The skateboarding park
Walk to John Street and (5) .... Walk straight down John Street until you get to Park Street. Go down Park Street and you will see the skateboarding park (6) .... you.

5 **Write instructions for how to get to the swimming pool.**

....
....
....

Exam tasks

Reading Part 3b

Complete the conversation between two friends.

What does Luke say to Cyndi?

Choose the correct letter **A–H**.

Cyndi: Hi, Luke. Did you come to school by car this morning?

Luke: **0** .....B.....

Cyndi: Why didn't you come on the bus?

Luke: **1** ....

Cyndi: Oh, did you get up late?

Luke: **2** ....

Cyndi: Oh dear! I always ride my bike to school.

Luke: **3** ....

Cyndi: When it's raining a lot my mum drives me.

Luke: **4** ....

Cyndi: It's a lorry! She works as a lorry driver.

Luke: **5** ....

Cyndi: Really? Come to school with us one morning!

A Fantastic! That's the job I want to do when I'm older.

B Yes, with my dad.

C Do you? Even in wet weather?

D What kind of car has she got?

E I usually do, but I missed it this morning.

F OK, does she cycle with you every morning?

G No, I forgot my homework, ran home to get it and the bus went without me.

H Yes, and then I woke up and had my breakfast with mum and dad.

Listening Part 2

17 Listen to Marcia talking to her friend, Josh, about taking the school bus.

Where does each person catch the school bus?

Write a letter **A–H** next to each person.

0 Josh [D]

	Friends	
1	Michael	[ ]
2	David	[ ]
3	Ellen	[ ]
4	Katy	[ ]
5	Tom	[ ]

	Places
A	traffic lights
B	bridge
C	car park
D	roundabout
E	tram stop
F	crossing
G	motorbike shop
H	cinema

Writing Part 7

Complete the email.

Write ONE word for each space.

From: Jodie

To: Bryony

Hi Bryony,

I **(0)** ....am.... glad you can come to the cinema on Saturday. The film starts either **(1)** .... 7.30 or 8.30. If you come to my house about 7 p.m., we can go to the earlier one together. I know you **(2)** .... not been to my new house in Mill Road before, but it's easy to find. It's **(3)** .... the left, opposite the café. It's older **(4)** .... any other house in the street and it's **(5)** .... tallest building there.

We can go to the cinema **(6)** .... tram. It only **(7)** .... five minutes from my house. After the film, **(8)** .... you like to stay with us for the night? I hope **(9)** ....! I downloaded some great music **(10)** .... afternoon just before I started writing this email. We can listen to that.

Jodie x

7 School rules!

Grammar

must / mustn't

1 Look at the school rules poster. Complete the sentences with *must* or *mustn't* and a verb from the box.

~~wear~~ talk use listen chew take eat put show ride

In the classroom

1 You must wear your school jacket and tie.
2 You .... to music on your MP3 player.
3 You .... chewing gum.
4 You .... pens, pencils and a ruler to your lessons.

In the library

5 You .... your mobile phones.
6 You .... food.
7 You .... to your friends.
8 You .... your library card to the librarian.

In the playground

9 You .... your bike.
10 You .... your rubbish in the bin.

2 Write four things you must and mustn't do in an exam.

You mustn't copy your friend's answers.
You must take some pens.

1 ....
2 ....
3 ....
4 ....

should / shouldn't

3 Match Peter's problems with the advice.

1 Peter is always hungry in the afternoon at school.
2 Peter often forgets what his homework is.
3 On rainy days, Peter's sweater is always wet.
4 Peter wants to play tennis better.
5 Peter is always tired in the morning.
6 Peter's sister is angry with him.

a He should write it down in a diary or notebook.
b He shouldn't borrow her things without asking.
c He should wear a jacket.
d He should eat more at lunchtime.
e He shouldn't go to bed late.
f He should take some lessons.

4 18 Listen and check your answers.

5 Complete the sentences. Use your own ideas.

1 Maria wants to learn to play the violin. She should take some lessons.
2 Paul wants to be healthier. He shouldn't ....
3 Franz wants to learn about sea animals. He should ....
4 Suzannah wants to make some new friends. She should ....
5 Anita wants to grow her hair long. She shouldn't ....
6 Henry doesn't like the colour of his bedroom walls. He should ....

can / could

6 Write sentences about Aysha.

Ability	Year she began
play basketball	2009
speak English	2008
surf	2011
swim	2006
ski	2010
play the keyboard	2009

1 play basketball / 2008
Aysha couldn't play basketball in 2008.
2 play basketball / 2010
Aysha could play basketball in 2010.
3 play basketball / now
Aysha can play basketball.
4 speak English / now
5 speak English / 2007
6 surf / 2010
7 surf / 2012
8 swim / 2008
9 ski / now
10 ski / 2009
11 play the keyboard / 2008

7 **Exam candidates often make mistakes with *can* and *could*. Correct one mistake in each of these sentences.**

1 The weather was nice so I ~~can~~ go everywhere.
could
2 I hope that next time you could come.
3 What a pity you can't come to my party because we went to play soccer.
4 I looked in the stores to see if I can find any souvenirs.
5 When he said this, I can't believe it!
6 I am so sorry that you couldn't came to the party.
7 My house is near Central Park so you will come on foot.
8 There the weather was cold and we coughtn't go to the swimming pool.
9 We can go to my house tomorrow and we can doing the homework.

Adverbs of manner

8 Choose the correct words.

1 I can't play table tennis very *well* / *good*.
2 We had to run *quick* / *quickly* to catch the bus.
3 Harry is *terrible* / *terribly* at Spanish.
4 Dave and Nick are learning French very *slow* / *slowly*.
5 Oliver sang his song *quiet* / *quietly*.
6 The classroom chairs are not very *comfortable* / *comfortably*.
7 After the exam, the students walked *happy* / *happily* out of the classroom.

Vocabulary

1 **Write the school subjects.**

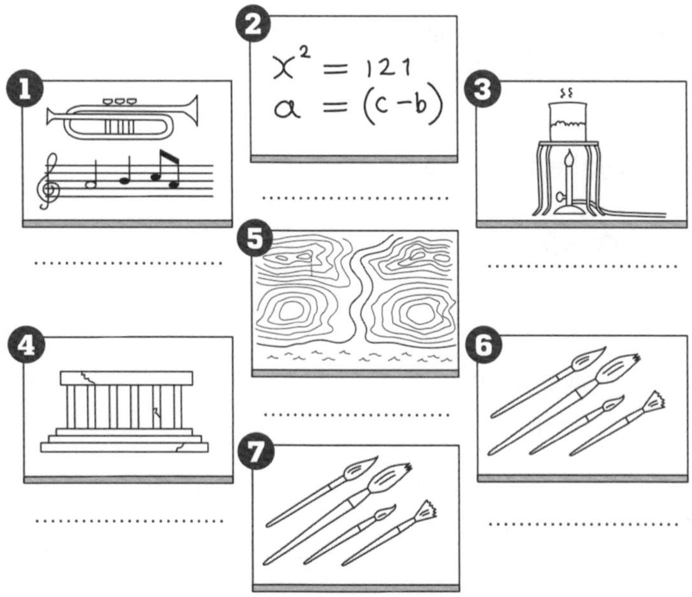

2 **Choose the correct words. Then write sentences for you.**

1 Hassan only *has* / *goes* lessons at school in the morning.
I have lessons in the morning and in the afternoon.
2 Hassan *studies* / *teaches* fourteen different subjects at school.
3 A man called Mr Ali *learns* / *teaches* Hassan maths.
4 Hassan *spends* / *uses* about two hours a night doing his homework.
5 Hassan has only *learned* / *missed* one day of school this school year.

3 19 **Listen and check your answers.**

4 Put the letters in the correct order to make instruments. Then match the instruments with the correct picture.

1 rumsd ..drums... [d]

2 tragiu .... [ ]

3 iolvni .... [ ]

4 bkoeyadr .... [ ]

5 niopa .... [ ]

Exam tasks

Reading Part 1

Which notice (**A–H**) says this (**1–5**)?

Choose the correct letter **A–H**.

0 Do not go quickly in this area. C

1 Your work must be easy to read.

2 Things have been more expensive here before now.

3 You must do activities quietly from this time.

4 Do not stand up when you are travelling on this.

5 You should do this fast if you can.

A Jarred Summer Camp
No loud music, TV or games after 10.00 p.m.

B Write your answers clearly on the exam answer sheet

C School car park
Drive slowly at all times

D Maze Music Shop
Check your change carefully before leaving

E Trains go past this platform very fast – stand behind the white line

F Please get on and off trains as quickly as possible

G Sit down – this bus may stop suddenly

H Kelly's Books
Today selling books more cheaply than ever!

Listening Part 5

20 You will hear a music teacher talking about her lessons.

Listen and complete each question.

After-school music lessons

Name of teacher:	Mrs Sweet
Instrument she teaches:	**(1)** ....
Day:	**(2)** ....
Room number:	**(3)** ....
Name of book to buy:	**(4)** ....
Price per month:	**(5)** £ ....

Writing Part 9

1 Exam candidates often make mistakes in Part 9 emails.

1 What is missing from the email?
2 Correct the underlined words.

Me, I like French music: Eddy Mitchell and Johnny Hallyday are my <u>prefers</u> French singers. I <u>like also</u> English music. The Beatles is the <u>goodest</u> group that I have ever <u>hear</u>. If you want, I can play the bass in the concert. I <u>a</u> going to <u>do</u> a meeting about the concert. Phone me on 3466 for more information <u>of</u> this. Thank you.

2 Read the email from your English friend, Nicky.

From: Nicky

To:

I love singing in my music lessons. What music do you play or listen to in lessons at school? What kind of music do you like best? What instrument would you like to learn at school?

Write an email to Nicky and answer the questions.

Write 25–35 words.

8 We had a great time!

Grammar

Past continuous

1 What were they doing at midnight on New Year's Eve? Write complete sentences.

1 
They were dancing at midnight on New Year's Eve ....

2 
He ....

3 
They ....

4 
They ....

5 
They ....

6 
She ....

7 ?
I ....

2 Write sentences about the people in Exercise 1 in the negative.

1 They / not sleep They weren't sleeping.
2 He / not dance ....
3 They / not study ....
4 They / not sing ....
5 They / not drink coffee ....
6 She / not laugh ....
7 I / not do an exam ....

Past simple & past continuous

3 Complete the sentences with the correct form of the verbs in brackets.

1 He .... (not stop) laughing while he .... (watch) the cartoon.
2 She .... (drop) the bowl on her foot while she .... (put) fruit in it.
3 They .... (see) the circus lorries in the street while they .... (walk) to school.
4 He .... (break) the light on his bike while he .... (try) to mend the wheel.
5 She .... (play) a computer game so she .... (not hear) the phone.
6 We .... (build) a fire for the first time while we .... (camp).

4 21 Listen and check your answers.

Vocabulary

1 Complete the words.

1 This is a large area of trees.
f o r e s t
2 People have holidays here in tents.
c _ _ _ _ _ _ _
3 This is the most important city in a country.
c _ _ _ _ _ _
4 When you do something very exciting it is one of these.
a _ _ _ _ _ _ _ _
5 You go to this place to sleep when you are not at home.
h _ _ _ _
6 It gives you information about places you visit.
g _ _ _ _ _ _ _ _
7 This place has water all around it.
i _ _ _ _ _

2 Choose the best word.

1 We all laughed when Dad fell over in the snow and he thought it was .... too.
a excellent (b) funny
2 I had a .... day because I met a friend and we went to the beach and had a lot of fun.
a wonderful b terrible
3 It was really .... to see the bear in the forest!
a tiring b exciting
4 The campsite was .... – there were no showers and only two toilets for twenty people!
a terrible b boring
5 I tried three different water sports yesterday so it was a .... day.
a tiring b boring
6 We loved the island that we stayed on because we saw lots of .... animals there.
a terrible b amazing

3 Put the words in the correct order.

1 nice wonderful not good
☹ not good .... 😐 nice .... ☺ wonderful ....
2 terrible OK bad
☹ .... ☹ .... 😐 ....
3 good amazing not bad
😐 .... ☺ .... ☺ ....
4 interesting boring all right
☹ .... 😐 .... ☺ ....
5 good brilliant OK
😐 .... ☺ .... ☺ ....
6 exciting boring good
☹ .... 😐 .... ☺ ....

Exam tasks

Listening Part 2

22 Listen to Matthew talking to his friend, Alice, about courses his friends took while they were on holiday.

Which course did each friend take?

For questions **1–5**, write a letter **A–H** next to each friend.

0 Alice D

	FRIENDS			COURSES
1	Ahmet		**A**	jewellery-making
2	Zena		**B**	language
3	Leah		**C**	cooking
4	Mick		**D**	writing
5	Ellie		**E**	science
			F	music
			G	water sports
			H	dance

Reading Part 4

Read about Katie Melua (a pop singer) and her holidays.

Then answer the questions.

Katie Melua: My holidays

My best holiday ever was staying in the Maldive Islands, at the Anantara Dhigu Hotel. We had a brilliant time doing water sports and eating in restaurants near the hotel after resting for a few days when we first got there. And the most exciting thing happened: my boyfriend asked me to marry him! We were walking along the beach one evening and he suddenly asked me! After the walk, we had a special dinner of fantastic fish and fruit dishes on the beach, but we were so excited that we couldn't eat much of it. We went and sat by the sea and watched some baby sharks in the water.

Last September we went to Cornwall, England after our wedding. I've been to Cornwall's beaches in the rain before, but we were lucky with the weather this time. While we were staying there, I decided to start surfing, so booked a lesson and loved it.

One of the worst things about travelling is losing your luggage. Once, my suitcase was lost on a flight to Germany. I was singing in a concert in Baden-Baden, which is famous for its natural hot baths. Unfortunately, it doesn't have many clothes shops! I had to borrow a friend's old jeans to wear while I was doing the show!

Holidays are good for a rest from work, and for learning new things. But ten days on holiday is usually long enough for me, then I want to get back to work.

0 What does Katie say about the Anantara Dhigu Hotel?
- **(A)** Her favourite holiday was there.
- **B** She always has good holidays there.
- **C** It's the nicest place in the Maldives.

1 During the first days of her holiday at the Anantara Dhigu Hotel, Katie
- **A** did outdoor activities.
- **B** rested a lot.
- **C** tried some restaurants.

2 Katie's boyfriend asked her to marry him
- **A** before their evening walk.
- **B** during their evening walk.
- **C** after their evening walk.

3 Katie didn't finish the meal she had on the beach because she
- **A** was given too many dishes.
- **B** felt too excited.
- **C** wanted to see some sharks.

4 What did Katie do for the first time last September?
- **A** She went surfing.
- **B** She visited Cornwall.
- **C** She had a rainy holiday.

5 Why did Katie go to Baden-Baden?
- **A** to try the natural baths
- **B** to go clothes shopping
- **C** to do her job

6 At the concert, Katie wore
- **A** a pair of her old jeans.
- **B** someone else's jeans.
- **C** jeans she bought in Germany.

7 Katie thinks that holidays should
- **A** be shorter than two weeks each time.
- **B** happen several times a year.
- **C** be in a new place every time.

Writing Part 8

Read the advertisement and the email.

Fill in the information in Jessica's notes.

Starbridge House
Dolphin Island's friendliest hotel!

Rooms per night
Family: £65
Double: £50

Airport to hotel – free taxi
Rented cars not available

Boat trips from hotel:
Shell Island (summer only)
High Town

Star Restaurant open all day
Book at www.hotelsite.com

From: Natasha
To: Jessica

It's great that your parents are taking you on holiday this autumn! This is the brilliant hotel we stay in – find out more from the hotel's own website, www.bridges.com. Don't stay in the double rooms, they're very small. You'll like Pizza Palace in Starbridge – the hotel food's a bit boring.

Jessica's Notes

Hotel

Island's name:	Dolphin
Travel from airport by:	1
Good place to eat:	2
Boat trip to:	3
Room price:	4 £
More information:	5 www

9 What's on?

Grammar

be going to

1 Match the sentence halves.

1 He's carrying his violin because
2 He's revising because
3 He's waiting in the street because
4 He's finding his seat in the theatre because
5 He's practising dancing because
6 He needs a knife because

a he's going to a disco later.
b he's going to cut the bread.
c he's going to play in a concert.
d a bus is going to come soon.
e the play is going to start soon.
f he's going to do an exam tomorrow.

2 23 Listen and check your answers.

3 Write questions with *going to* and the words in brackets.

1 Those children look excited. (see the circus?) ....Are they going to see the circus?...
2 You're going to bed early. (get up early tomorrow?) ....
3 She's carrying an umbrella. (it / rain?) ....
4 He's reading a guidebook about Portugal. (go / Portugal?) ....
5 You can't go to the cinema this evening. (go / basketball practice?) ....
6 The train is going more slowly now. (it / stop soon?) ....
7 You've put the plates, knives and forks on the table. (we / have dinner soon?) ....

Infinitives & *-ing* forms

4 Complete the sentences with the correct form of the verb in brackets.

1 The guitarist would like ....to play......... (play) in a famous band.
2 The photographer hopes .... (take) some good pictures of the mountains today.
3 The actor is very good at .... (speak) like other people.
4 The artist thinks it is difficult .... (find) a good place for an exhibition of her art.
5 The journalist is interested in .... (write) an article about circus children.
6 The dancer enjoys .... (practise) his dance outside.
7 The drummer doesn't mind .... (sit) behind the other musicians in the band.

Vocabulary

1 What arts event are they going to? Write the words.

1	Harry is going to the cinema.	a f.ilm.......
2	Dana is going to watch people act in a theatre.	a p...........
3	Ed is going to watch a band playing.	a c...........
4	George is going to watch some clowns.	a c...........
5	Kate is going to dance to pop music with her friends.	a d...........
6	Simon is going to look at some photos and paintings.	an e...........

2 Match the programmes with the descriptions below.

1 cartoon
2 the news
3 quiz show
4 sports programme
5 music programme

		Channel 21
a	**3.00 p.m.**	Two teams of teenagers answer questions about history, art and science. The best team wins a trip to Peru.
b	**3.30 p.m.**	Funny dinosaur Matty plays amazing games with his new friend Mouse.
c	**3.45 p.m.**	Leona Lewis in concert in Frankfurt.
d	**4.00 p.m.**	Learn what's happened today from our journalists around the world.
e	**4.15 p.m.**	Match between Manchester United and Real Madrid.

3 Answer the questions.

1	Is a singer a musician or a journalist?	a musician
2	Is a journalist a writer or a dancer?	....
3	Is a guitarist an actor or a musician?	....
4	Is a painter an actor or an artist?	....
5	Is a drummer a musician or a writer?	....
6	Is a film star an actor or a journalist?	....
7	Is a pop star a singer or a painter?	....
8	Is a photographer a musician or an artist?	....

Exam tasks

Reading Part 3b

Complete the conversation between two friends.

What does Aiden say to Paul?

Choose the correct letter **A–H**.

Aiden: Have you ever been to the music festival in Heaton Village?

Paul: .....C.....

Aiden: No, never. But I'd like to go. It's next week.

Paul: **1** ....

Aiden: Every sort. There's a hip-hop artist on Saturday afternoon. Would you like to see him with me?

Paul: **2** ....

Aiden: OK, how about coming to the festival disco next Friday evening, then?

Paul: **3** ....

Aiden: So when are you free next week?

Paul: **4** ....

Aiden: That's brilliant because a great rock guitarist is playing that night.

Paul: **5** ....

Aiden: OK, I can book them online.

A Really? What kind of music is played there?

B I'm busy every evening except Thursday.

C No. What about you?

D Good idea! Saturday is better for me.

E I'm not sure. I don't like that kind of music.

F I'm sorry, no. I hate dancing and I've got football practice.

G Cool! Let's get some tickets.

H That's wonderful. We can dance to the music.

Listening Part 4

24 You will hear Neil talking to his friend about an art exhibition.

Listen and complete each question.

Art club exhibition

Name of exhibition:	Young Artists
Type of art:	paintings and **(1)** ....
Date exhibition opens:	**(2)** .... July
Place:	**(3)** ....
Cost of paintings:	**(4)** between £7.50 and £.....................................
Subject of lessons:	**(5)** ....

Writing Part 9

1 Complete the email with *and*, *but*, *because* and *or*.

From: Paddy

To: James

Hi James,

How are you? Did you go out last night? I wanted to see a film yesterday (1) .... there was nothing on that I wanted to see. Next week there are some good new films, though. 'Gone Tomorrow' (2) .... also 'High Seas' will be on in both the cinemas in town. Do you like the cinema in Castle Street (3) .... the one in French Street best? I prefer the one in Castle Street (4) .... the seats are more comfortable. Do you want to see one of these films with me on Wednesday evening?

See you soon,

Paddy

2 Your friend Paddy asked you to go to the cinema with him.

Write a message to Paddy.

Say:

- **why** you can't go on Wednesday
- **when** you would like to go
- **which** film you want to see.

Write **25–35** words.

10 Are you an outdoors person?

Grammar

will / won't and *may*

1 Complete the sentences with *will*, *won't* or *may*.

1 We're staying on an island where it's always sunny so I ...won't... take my scarf and gloves.
2 Let's try this path – it .... go to the car park. I hope so anyway!
3 There's going to be a bad storm this evening so I've decided I .... go for a run.
4 It .... rain today because it's cloudy, but I'm not sure.
5 I .... wear my warm coat to school because it's so cold.
6 We .... walk to the top of the hill because we haven't got time.

First conditional

2 Complete the sentences with the correct form of the verbs in brackets.

1 She ...'ll go... (go) to the lake with Nick if he .doesn't have. (not have) football practice.
2 If she .... (go) to the lake, she .... (need) her swimming costume.
3 If she .... (take) a picnic, she .... (not need) to buy food in the café.
4 If she .... (cycle) around the lake, she .... (feel) tired.
5 If she .... (see) some interesting animals, she .... (take) photos of them.
6 She .... (put) her camera in her bag if it .... (start) to rain.
7 She .... (not take) her rain jacket if the weather .... (be) good.

3 25 Listen and check your answers.

4 Exam candidates often make mistakes with the first conditional. Correct one mistake in each sentence.

1 ~~I'm~~ the happiest girl in the world if I find it. I'll be
2 I am sure when I go back home I am fat.
3 If you like we would go by car.
4 If I can I am going.
5 We will pick you up from the airport when you'll arrive at about 10.30 a.m. on the 20th of June.
6 If you need some information about these studies, you would not find it here. You need to look online.

Vocabulary

1 Where are they? Use the places in the box.

~~on a farm~~	in a wood	on a river	in a field
on a hill	by a gate	on a path	on a lake

1 I'm staying here with my uncle. He's got cows, chickens and two horses. ...on a farm...
2 I'm on a boat tour, travelling around Paris. ....
3 There are lots of sheep eating grass here and a gate in one corner of it. ....
4 It's great walking on this because no cars or bikes can use it – it's not wide enough. ....
5 I couldn't open it so I had to climb over it. ....
6 Wow! I'm at the top and I can see villages and the countryside below me. ....
7 I'm lost because all the trees here look the same! ....
8 There are trees all around it and we're sailing across it. ....

2 Label the pictures, then write the correct season next to each sentence.

1 It looks hot. ..summer..
2 There aren't any clouds in the sky. ....
3 There is snow on the hills. ....
4 The clouds are dark so it may rain soon. ....
5 It looks very cold. ....
6 There are a few green leaves on the trees. ....
7 Leaves are falling off the trees. ....

3 Label the pictures then write the words in the correct place in the puzzle.

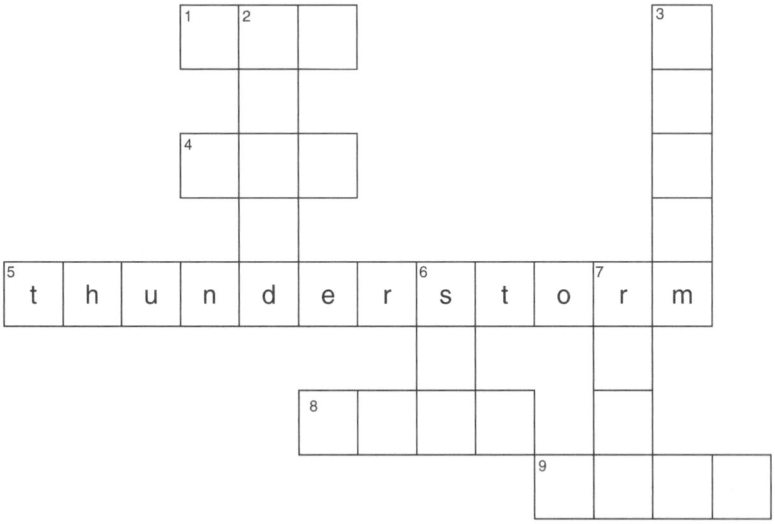

a  ....

b  ....

c  ....

d 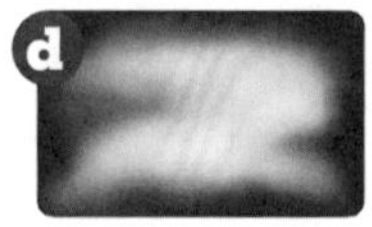 ....

e  ....

f  ....

g  ....

h  ....

i  ....

Exam tasks

Writing Part 8

Read the advertisement and the email.

Fill in the information in Martin's notes.

Day in North Wood

Learn about
animals and trees
Teachers: Jane Williams, Mike Moon

Buses from:
Hill Street 9.15 a.m.
River Street 9.30 a.m.

Only £8.50
Students free

From: Andy
To: Martin

Let's go to the wood day together. We should take the earlier bus – it goes from nearer our houses. I looked online – it comes back at 5 p.m., and only stops at the station. Jane Williams won't be there. Pity, she taught us great lessons at school last week. The ground may be wet, so we'll need boots. But no mobile phones!

Martin's Notes
Day out

Name of wood:	North
Bus time:	1 .... a.m.
Teacher's name:	2
Take:	3
Cost:	4
Bus returns to:	5

Listening Part 1

26 You will hear five short conversations.

There is one question for each conversation.

For each question, choose the right answer (**A**, **B** or **C**).

1 What was the weather like last winter?

A

B

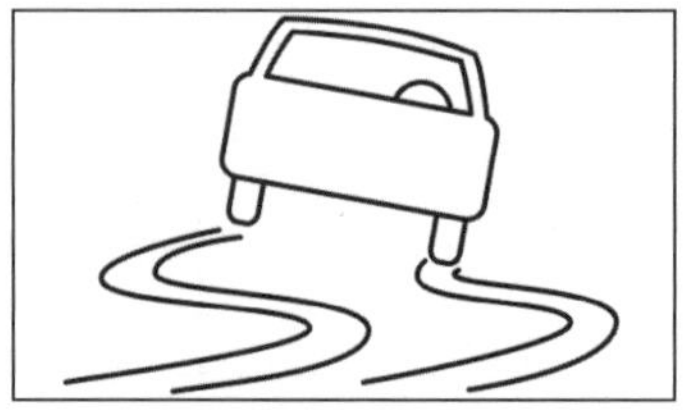
C

2 Who will go for the birthday meal with Jade and her parents?

A

B

C

3 What happened during the storm last week?

A

B

C

4 What work does Eleanor do on the farm at weekends?

A

B

C

5 Where is Richard's MP3 player?

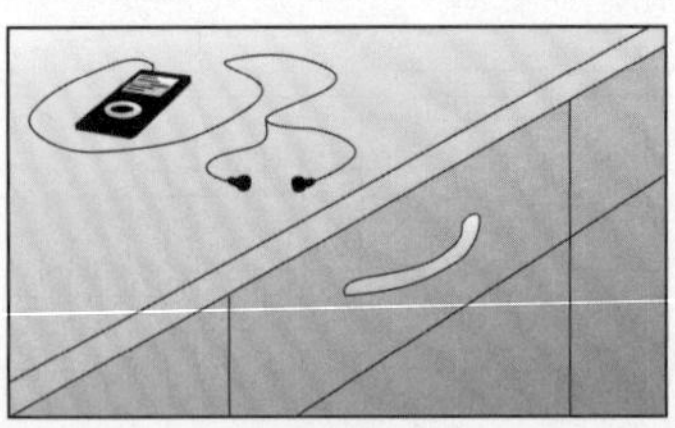
A

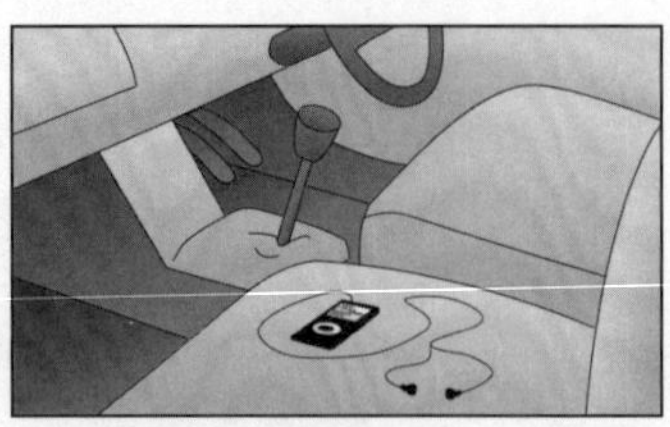
B

C

Reading Part 1

Which notice (**A–H**) says this (**1–5**)?

Choose the correct letter **A–H**.

0 Do not leave this open. C

1 If you want to do this activity, you must join a group.

2 Some walkers pay more to come here than others.

3 You cannot go into this place through here.

4 Cars and bicycles must not go on these.

5 Do not cook food outside here.

A

Midbank Forest Map
Red forest paths are for walkers only.

B

Aged 12–16? Do our 'Food from Nature' quiz and win prizes

C

Please remember to close the gate

D

Jarrett Wood
No fires or barbecues

E

Sandilane Farm
No entry – use gate in next field

F

Fishing in this lake is for members of Bluevale Club only

G

Hill-walking club car park
All day £4.50
Members £1.00

H

Green River rent-a-boat (per person)
½ hour: £3.50 **1 hour: £5.00**

11 Healthy body, healthy mind

Grammar

Present perfect; *just / yet / already*

1 Complete the questions with the correct form of the verbs in brackets. Then write true short answers.

Have you ever ...

1 ..bought.. (buy) a newspaper?
No, I haven't.
2 .... (fly) in a helicopter?
3 .... (take) a photo of a pet?
4 .... (catch) a fish?
5 .... (go) to the Taj Mahal?
6 .... (see) a white rabbit?
7 .... (be) in a school play?
8 .... (do) your homework on a bus?
9 .... (hear) yourself speaking on a recording?
10 .... (eat) an insect?

2 Complete the conversation with *just*, *yet* or *already*.

Dad: Hi Adam. What are you doing?
Adam: I've (1) ...just.... got home from my music lesson. Have you had dinner (2) .... ?
Dad: No, not (3) ....
Adam: I'm hungry. Do you want me to help you cook?
Dad: No, I've (4) .... done it. I prepared the fish this morning and cooked it earlier this evening.
Adam: Great! Let's eat. I'll put the knives and forks on the table.
Dad: I've (5) .... done that, a minute ago. But I haven't put any water or glasses on the table (6) .... Can you do that, please?
Adam: OK.

3 27 Listen and check your answers.

4 Complete the sentences with the correct form of these verbs.

~~start~~ drink not eat sit not finish read win

1 It ....has............ just ....started......... to rain so I'm going inside.
2 We're very happy because we .... all our matches this autumn.
3 They .... lunch yet because they're still cooking it.
4 She .... just .... a whole bottle of water because the run made her very thirsty.
5 Stand up quickly! You .... just .... on my glasses!
6 He .... his homework yet because his friend phoned while he was doing it.
7 I won't borrow that book because I .... already .... it.

Present perfect with *for* & *since*

5 Write two sentences for each prompt using *for* and *since*.

1 I / not see Frankie / two months / April
I haven't seen Frankie for two months.
I haven't seen Frankie since April.
2 He / be / a waiter / 2012 / two years
....
....
3 The cat / not eat anything / Tuesday / two days
....
....
4 We / live in this house / nine years / 2005
....
....
5 I / have this bike / I was twelve years old / five years
....
....
6 She / be in the shop / an hour / three o'clock
....
....

Vocabulary

1 Put the letters in the correct order to complete the sentences.

1 Cats have four **e s g l**. legs
2 At the dentist's you have to open your **o t h m u**.
3 We have four fingers on each **n a d h**.
4 New babies don't have any **e t e t h**.
5 Horses don't have any **s a m r**.
6 Some men have a beard on their **a c e f**.
7 When you sleep you close your **y e e s**.
8 If you eat too much, you will get a big **a c s o t m h**.
9 Old people have grey or white **r h i a**.
10 You sit on a horse's **a k c b**.

2 Label the faces with these words.

~~afraid~~ angry glad thirsty hungry unhappy sorry sick tired

a

....afraid........

b

....

c

....

d

....

e

....

f

....

g

....

h

....

i

....

Exam tasks

Reading Part 5

Read the article about a girl's headache medicine.

Choose the best word (**A**, **B** or **C**) for each space.

My medicine for headaches

I have **(0)** .... returned from a holiday in the mountains of Peru. I went **(1)** .... with my family. My parents have **(2)** .... me on other holidays in mountain areas, but the mountains in Peru were the highest I've **(3)** .... seen.

One day, **(4)** .... I was looking around a very old village, I started to talk to an old woman. I told her I had a headache **(5)** .... we were so high up in the mountains. She went to a plant **(6)** .... was growing near us, took a **(7)** .... flowers from it and gave some to me. She told me to smell them. They smelt **(8)** .... the tea my mum sometimes drinks at home. It was a lovely smell. And then my head stopped hurting. It was amazing!

0	**A** nearly	(**B**) just	**C** yet
1	**A** walked	**B** walk	**C** walking
2	**A** take	**B** took	**C** taken
3	**A** ever	**B** never	**C** before
4	**A** after	**B** while	**C** during
5	**A** because	**B** but	**C** or
6	**A** who	**B** where	**C** which
7	**A** lot	**B** few	**C** bit
8	**A** with	**B** as	**C** like

Writing Part 6

Read the descriptions of some adjectives about feelings.

What is the word for each one?

The first letter is already there. There is one space for each other letter in the word.

0 This is how you feel in your stomach when you are ill. s i c k

1 This is another word for sad. u _ _ _ _ _ _

2 When you want a drink you feel like this. t _ _ _ _ _ _

3 You feel this when something nice happens. g _ _ _

4 You are this when you need to have a rest. t _ _ _ _

5 If you need food, you feel like this. h _ _ _ _ _

Reading Part 3a

Complete the five conversations.

Choose **A**, **B** or **C**.

0 

Where are you from?

Ⓐ London.

B Home.

C The train station.

1 What's the matter?

A It's a kind of tooth.

B Is it my tooth?

C My tooth hurts.

2 Has she seen the doctor?

A Not now.

B Not yet.

C Not then.

3 I've got a temperature and a headache.

A Why don't you go and lie down?

B Really? You're bored.

C Are you feeling better?

4 How did Kate break her arm?

A She fell on some ice.

B After basketball practice.

C I know, it was terrible.

5 Thanks for looking after me when I was ill.

A Never mind.

B Of course.

C You're welcome.

Listening Part 3

28 Listen to Christina talking to her friend Barney about her health problem.

For each question, choose the right answer (**A**, **B**, or **C**).

0 Christina has hurt her
- **A** neck.
- Ⓑ back.
- **C** arm.

1 When is Christina going to see the doctor?
- **A** today
- **B** tomorrow
- **C** next Thursday

2 Christina fell over when she was
- **A** going up some stairs.
- **B** practising basketball.
- **C** walking to school.

3 Where is Christina now?
- **A** in her bedroom
- **B** in her living room
- **C** in her kitchen

4 Christina is unhappy because she cannot
- **A** play her guitar.
- **B** skateboard.
- **C** go swimming.

5 Christina would like to read Barney's book about
- **A** a film star.
- **B** a pop star.
- **C** a sports star.

12 Technology & me

Grammar

The passive: present

1 Complete the information with the present passive form of the verbs in brackets.

FACTFILE

YouTube Amazing information about YouTube

1 Every day, 4,000,000,000 videos *are watched* (watch) on YouTube.
2 Sixty hours of video .... (put) on YouTube every minute.
3 Each month, YouTube .... (visit) by 800 million visitors all around the world.
4 Something .... (write) about the videos by about 50% of visitors to YouTube.
5 Over 700 YouTube videos .... (share) on Twitter each minute.
6 YouTube videos .... (see) on mobile phones over 600 million times a day.
7 Over 3,000,000,000 hours .... (spent) watching videos on YouTube each month.

The passive: past

2 Write past passive sentences. Use *on*, *in*, *of* or *by*.

1 The first email / send / 1971
The first email was sent in 1971.
2 The first digital cameras / sell / a company called Logitech
....
3 The first fridge / build / Jacob Perkins / 1834
....
4 The first computer mouse / make / wood
....
5 The first hairdryer / use / a French hairdresser
....
6 The first text messages / write / 3rd December 1992
....

3 29 Listen and check your answers.

Vocabulary

1 Label the pictures then write the words in the correct place in the puzzle.

a 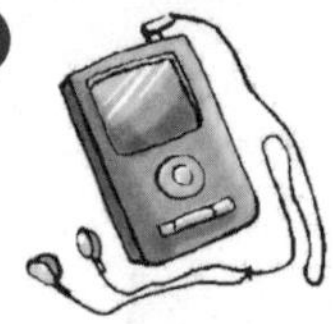
....

b 
....

c 
....

d 
....

e 
....

f 
....

g 
....

h 
....

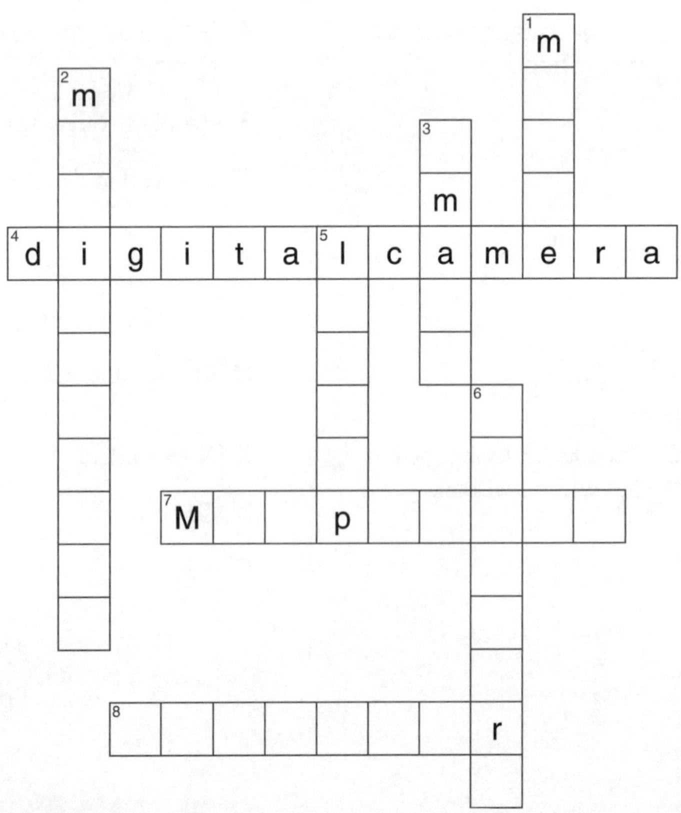

2 Put the letters in the correct order to make technology words.

1 Yesterday, I **loadeddown** some great songs from an online music store. downloaded.
2 What is your **malie dressda**? I want to write to you. ....
3 Menus are usually at the top of your computer **encres**. ....
4 Send me a **xett** when you get to the station. ....
5 Do you use your computer to **cath** to your friends? ....
6 You can take a **toplap** to work or play on when you are travelling. ....
7 If you **klicc** on the cross, the box will close. ....
8 There are some great science websites on the **netterin**. ....

3 Match the sentence halves.

1	A lamp is used	**a**	to carry things in.
2	A case is used	**b**	to dry your hair.
3	A fridge is used	**c**	to read at night.
4	A keyboard is used	**d**	to tell you the time.
5	A clock is used	**e**	to write on a computer.
6	A hairdryer is used	**f**	to keep food cold.

Exam tasks

Listening Part 2

30 Listen to Alice talking to her mum about finding things on the Internet.

What thing does each person want to find?

For questions 1–5 write a letter **A–H** next to each person.

0 Aunt [C]

	FRIENDS			**THINGS**
1	Dad	[ ]	**A**	film
2	Brother	[ ]	**B**	camera
3	Sister	[ ]	**C**	hairdryer
4	Cousin	[ ]	**D**	mobile phone
5	Grandma	[ ]	**E**	printer
			F	TV
			G	instrument
			H	laptop

Reading Part 4

Read the article about young people who've made computer games for a competition. Then answer the questions.

Charlotte

I learned to make games at school in IT and art lessons when I was ten. We made video cartoons. I worked on the game for this competition at school, too. Last year, my brother and I made a different game for a school competition and we won a trip to a computer games company with one of the teachers. When I leave school I'd love to work there, but I don't think I'll earn a lot.

Abigail

I made the game for fun for my brother. I planned to make a different one for the games competition. However, when I showed it to my IT teacher at school, he thought it was brilliant and said I should enter it! Everyone just loves playing it. I'm really excited about the competition, but I don't think I'm going to win. In the future, I want to start my own technology company.

Françoise

When I was eleven I played video games all the time. So I began to try new video games for a computer games company. We had to play them and find any problems and I earned money for doing it. I also started to get ideas and I began to make the game I'm entering for the competition. I've always worked hard and I usually pass all my art, IT, business and maths exams at school easily. I hope to do a course in computer art at college next year.

0 Who made a game for a member of her family?

A Charlotte (**B**) Abigail **C** Françoise

1 Who has already won a prize in a competition?

A Charlotte **B** Abigail **C** Françoise

2 Who is good at several subjects at school?

A Charlotte **B** Abigail **C** Françoise

3 Who was paid to check new computer games when she was younger?

A Charlotte **B** Abigail **C** Françoise

4 Who was given advice about the competition by a teacher?

A Charlotte **B** Abigail **C** Françoise

5 Who has made films during school time?

A Charlotte **B** Abigail **C** Françoise

6 Who wants to get a job with a computer games company?

A Charlotte **B** Abigail **C** Françoise

7 Who is planning to do more studying after she's left school?

A Charlotte **B** Abigail **C** Françoise

Writing Part 7

Complete the emails.

Write ONE word for each space.

From: Pippa
To: Tracey

Hi Tracey,

Can I come and use your printer **(0)** ...*this*.... evening? Dad bought one online last week but it **(1)** .... not arrived yet. I want **(2)** .... print about six photos. They **(3)** .... taken by Mum when I went snowboarding – it was **(4)** .... best holiday I've ever had!

Pippa x

From: Tracey
To: Pippa

Hi Pippa

(5) .... course you can use my printer. It's a bit slow **(6)** .... it prints good pictures. **(7)** .... don't you come at 6.00 p.m.? You can eat dinner **(8)** .... us before we print the photos. It will **(9)** .... interesting to see them! When **(10)** .... your dad think the printer will arrive?

Tracey x

Vocabulary extra

1 My family, my friends & me

1 Look at the photo and write the correct names.

1 Write *Sara's grandmother, Sara's father, Sara's brother, Sara's mother* next to the right people.

2 Write these words below: *aunts, grandfather, son, daughter, cousins.*

- **a** Sara's grandmother's husband = her ....
- **b** Sara's parents' sisters = her ....
- **c** Sara's uncle's children = her ....
- **d** Sara's brother = her parents' ....
- **e** Sara = her parents' ....

2 Underline one word that is different.

1	eye	snack	hair	face
2	slim	short	tall	thirsty
3	fat	curly	long	straight
4	towel	purse	money	bank
5	favourite	best	nice	terrible
6	dark	yellow	brown	fair
7	dictionary	pencil	diary	notebook

2 In my free time

1 Match the parts of the phrases. Then number the six pictures.

1	play	**a**	stamps
2	draw	**b**	films
3	cook a	**c**	songs
4	take	**d**	in a tent
5	listen to	**e**	sports
6	sleep	**f**	photos
7	play an	**g**	at a disco
8	play computer	**h**	meal
9	go	**i**	pictures
10	watch	**j**	instrument
11	collect	**k**	games
12	dance	**l**	to a concert

3 Eating in, eating out

1 Label the picture with words from the box. You don't need all the words.

cupboard sofa toilet chair cooker shower bed table mirror lamp shelf floor ceiling fridge desk

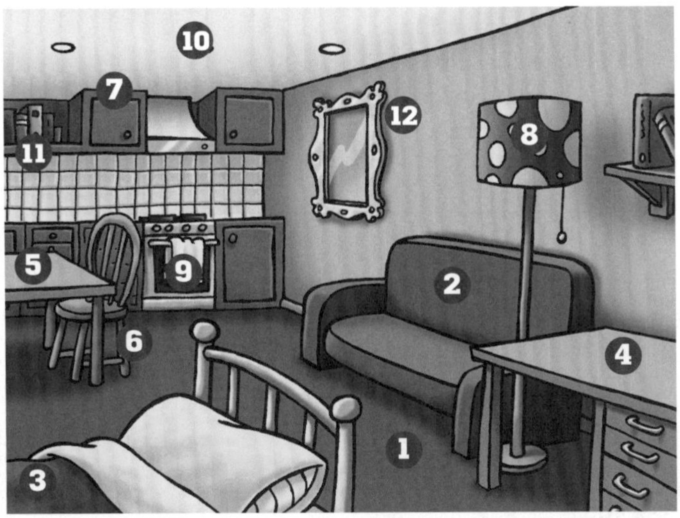

1	....	5	....	9	....
2	....	6	....	10	....
3	....	7	....	11	....
4	....	8	....	12	....

2 Find 12 food and drink words. Then write the words below.

D	E	C	H	I	C	K	E	N	P
F	I	S	T	S	C	L	E	M	O
B	T	S	S	C	H	E	B	E	J
P	J	U	A	I	D	A	R	C	U
O	M	E	L	E	T	T	E	H	I
T	I	Y	A	X	S	A	A	E	C
A	M	L	D	W	O	F	D	E	E
T	U	O	P	W	U	I	Q	S	G
O	N	I	O	N	P	S	L	E	R
R	R	I	C	E	T	H	J	A	M

1 This is a type of meat. ....
2 These are types of vegetables. .... , ...
3 You catch it in the sea. ....
4 You make it with vegetables or meat. ....
5 You make it with eggs. ....
6 You make them with fruit. .... , ...
7 You make dishes like paella and risotto with it. ....
8 You make it from milk. ....
9 You make it with flour. ....
10 This often has lettuce and tomatoes in it. ....

4 What are you doing now?

1 Write sports in the grey squares to complete the puzzle. Use the pictures to help you.

2 Put the letters in the correct order to make words for clothes.

1 tishrT ..T-shirt..
2 swmimgin stmecuo ....
3 sotob ....
4 rantrise ....
5 osrutrse ....
6 rfsac ....
7 ktcjae ....
8 sdesr ....
9 astrwee ....
10 hosse ....
11 hsotrs ....
12 mehlte ....
13 tcoa ....
14 anejs ....
15 csoks ....
16 ktrsi ....

5 Great places to visit

1 Match the activities with the places.

1 watching a film
2 looking at things that are very old
3 being a student
4 buying a magazine
5 asking for help when something is stolen
6 buying some clothes, a handbag and a mirror
7 watching a play
8 buying a dictionary
9 finding a book to borrow

a a university
b a newsagent
c a library
d a department store
e a police station
f a cinema
g a theatre
h a museum
i a bookshop

2 Complete the tables.

1	1st	first
4		
9		
11		
12		
31		
25		
18		

Write	**Say**
May 12th	May the twelfth
27th January	
	the sixteenth of August
	the twenty-third of February, two thousand and one
July 13th, 2008	
22nd December, 1994	
	April the tenth, eighteen eighty-seven

6 Getting there

1 Choose the correct word to complete the sentences.

1 *Bikes / Ships* sail across the sea.
2 A whole class can go on a school trip in a *taxi / coach*.
3 The *plane / underground* is a good way of getting around a city.
4 You can fly across a country in a *train / helicopter*.
5 In very bad weather, riding a *tram / motorbike* is not a good idea.
6 *Lorries / Boats* carry things around countries by road.

2 Label the signs with words from the box. You don't need all the words.

park road square car park traffic lights roundabout crossing bridge corner

1 ....

2 ....

3 ....

4 ....

5 ....

6 ....

7 School rules!

1 Match two activities with each subject.

studying mountains and rivers
studying how plants grow
reading about past events
painting
learning grammar rules
learning about past kings and queens
playing an instrument

art
history
music
science
English
geography
maths

learning about how to find the size of triangles
drawing
adding numbers
learning about weather in different countries
singing
learning about space
doing a listening test

2 Label the instruments.

1 k................ **2** v................ **3** p................ **4** d................ **5** g................

8 We had a great time!

1 Look at the photo. Complete the questions and answers with these words.

trying	speaking	climbing	having	staying	visiting

1 What is he doing?
He's ....

2 What kind of places does he like ....?
Places with lots of mountains.

3 Where is he ....?
At a campsite near the mountain.

4 Why isn't he going up the mountain at the moment?
He's .... a rest.

5 What languages is he good at ....?
German and Italian.

6 What is he doing tomorrow?
He's .... a new adventure sport.

2 Choose the correct word to complete the sentences.

1 I didn't enjoy that book. It was too long and ....boring..... . *boring / exciting*

2 We had a really .... time. We learned how to sail a small boat. *terrible / amazing*

3 Sorry I didn't phone. The journey home was .... so I went to bed early. *tiring / wonderful*

4 That restaurant was .... I couldn't eat the meat and the chips were cold. *terrible / excellent*

5 The science museum is really .... You can learn a lot of new things there. *boring / interesting*

6 The hotel was .... It had a swimming pool, a cinema and shops. *funny / brilliant*

9 What's on?

1 Where did these people go? There is one extra word.

a concert	an exhibition	a play	a festival	a disco	a party	a circus	a film

1 There were about 50 pictures, all painted by children. ....

2 It was at Robert's house, and all my friends were there. It was good fun. ....

3 It was quite expensive to enter, and it was OK, but not many people danced. I don't think the music was right. ....

4 Everyone in the band played so well, and the singing was brilliant. ....

5 I didn't think the clowns were very funny. ....

6 I loved it and all the actors are amazing. But we sat very close to the screen, so my neck hurts now! ....

7 We sat at the front of the theatre, so we were very near the actors. ....

2 Are the sentences true (T) or false (F)?

1 Cartoons are usually very sad.
2 You watch the weather to find out if it's going to rain.
3 The news usually makes you laugh a lot.
4 People sometimes win lots of money in quiz shows.
5 Music programmes are usually for people aged 70 and over.
6 Only people who are good at sports watch sports programmes.

10 Are you an outdoors person?

1 In which picture can you see these things? Write A, B, or A & B.

A

B

1 a gate ....
2 some hills ....
3 a river ....
4 a wood ....
5 some fields ....
6 a lake ....
7 a farm ....
8 a path ....

2 Find 12 weather and seasons words.

W	U	C	I	W	K	L	A	F	O	G	G
I	B	L	A	I	T	F	A	G	O	H	S
N	M	O	P	N	E	A	V	S	U	M	U
T	H	U	N	D	E	R	S	T	O	R	M
E	A	D	C	R	R	J	P	I	T	F	M
R	A	I	N	F	S	A	R	N	S	M	E
O	T	R	A	I	M	C	I	L	U	L	R
K	F	S	N	O	W	O	N	E	N	E	X
I	C	E	T	R	W	Q	G	M	J	O	P
A	S	Y	J	A	U	T	U	M	N	K	O

11 Healthy body, healthy mind

1 Are the sentences true (T) or false (F)? Correct the false sentences.

1 You see with your ears.
2 Your face shows if you are happy or not.
3 You put shoes on your feet.
4 A dentist helps you look after your teeth.
5 People have two noses.
6 Eyes can be blue, green or brown.
7 Your neck is at the end of your legs.
8 You put food in your mouth to eat it.
9 You wear a hat on your stomach.
10 People have three legs.
11 You can hold things in your hands.
12 You wear necklaces on your arms.

2 Match the sentence halves.

What's the matter?

1 I burnt my mouth because I
2 I went to the dentist because I
3 I put a plaster on my finger because I
4 I want to lie down somewhere quiet because I
5 I feel very hot because I
6 I'm not hungry because I

a have got a headache.
b have got a temperature.
c drank some hot tea.
d had toothache.
e have got a stomach ache.
f cut it.

12 Technology & me

1 Write the words, then match the things to the correct picture.

1 h_ _ _d_ _ _r
2 M_ _ p_ _ _ _r
3 d_ _ _ _ _l c_ _ _ _a
4 m_ _ _e
5 k_ _ _ _ _ _ _

6 g_ _ _ _ c_ _ _ _ _e
7 l_ _ _ _ _
8 m_ _ _ _ _ p_ _ _ _
9 p_ _ _ _ _r
10 a_ _ _ _ c_ _ _ _

2 Tick (✓) the correct verbs. You can tick more than one box for each item.

write	chat	play	text	watch	download	call	send	
				✓				TV
								on a mobile phone
								a computer game
								a film from the internet
								a message
								an email
								to friends online

Audio scripts

Unit 1

Vocabulary, Exercise 2 Track 1

1 I've got one brother but I haven't got any sisters.
2 I am my parents' only daughter.
3 My aunt Diana is married to my uncle Jacob.
4 Diana and Jacob have got two sons, Ben and Joe. Ben and Joe are my favourite cousins.
5 My aunt Katie hasn't got a husband – she doesn't want to get married yet.
6 My grandparents (my mum's mother and father) are both 65 years old.
7 My grandfather is one month younger than my grandmother.

Vocabulary, Exercise 4 Track 2

1 Daisy has got a pair of trainers to wear for a basketball lesson.
2 Freddie has got some pencils for drawing pictures.
3 Daisy has got a diary to write homework in.
4 Freddie has got a mobile to call mum at lunchtime.
5 Daisy has got some money in a blue purse.
6 Freddie has got a snack because teenagers are always hungry!
7 Daisy has got a towel for a swimming lesson.

Listening Part 3 Track 3

Listen to Kelly talking to her mum about her violin lessons. For each question, choose the right answer (A, B or C).

Woman: Kelly, I've just spoken to your violin teacher. You haven't got a lesson this week.
Girl: Is she ill, Mum?
Woman: No, she's on a course because she's doing an exam next month.
Girl: So when's my next lesson?
Woman: It'll be the 15th – you're missing this week, the 8th August, and on the 22nd, your teacher's away again.
Girl: Right.
Woman: She said you need a new music book, too.
Girl: Oh, OK. Where can we get that?
Woman: Well, they haven't got any music at the library, I've looked before. The bookshop's cheaper than the music shop, so we'll get it there.
Girl: OK. Which day?
Woman: How about Thursday? Not tomorrow, I work late on Tuesdays and you've got dance club on Wednesday.
Girl: Fine. Will you pick me up after school?
Woman: No, I'll only finish work at quarter to four, so go home first. I'll pick you up there at four o'clock. Then we'll get to the shop about quarter past four.
Girl: Right. Can we have our dinner in a café afterwards?
Woman: OK. You know the burger restaurant's closed, but we can go and have a pizza. The fish café's too far from the shops.
Girl: Great!

Unit 2

Grammar, Exercise 4 Track 4

Julian: Did you go to Music Club yesterday?
Peter: No, they played jazz and I don't like jazz much.
Julian: What kind of music do you like?
Peter: Rock, pop, classical – most kinds, but not jazz!
Julian: I'd like to come too. Can I just come or do I have to ask the teacher first?
Peter: Just come when you want to. Would you like to come with me next week?
Julian: Yes, please. I'd like to join so I can learn to play an instrument.
Peter: Do you like all kinds of music?
Julian: I like modern music best, but I'd like to learn more about classical and jazz, too.
Peter: Music Club will be perfect for you!

Vocabulary, Exercise 4 Track 5

1 Ellie loves watching films. Maisie hates watching films.
2 Ellie hates cooking. Maisie loves cooking.
3 Ellie enjoys singing. Maisie doesn't like singing.
4 Ellie likes going to concerts. Maisie doesn't enjoy going to concerts.
5 Ellie is very good at playing computer games. Maisie is terrible at playing computer games.
6 Ellie likes dancing more than doing sports. Maisie prefers doing sports to dancing.
7 Ellie thinks history is boring. Maisie is interested in history.

Listening Part 4, Exercise 1 Track 6

Narrator: One
Girl: Which day does Stamp Club meet this week?
Boy: On Thursday.
Narrator: Two
Boy: When do you usually go shopping?
Girl: On Saturdays.
Narrator: Three
Girl: How do you spell your surname?
Boy: C-A-P-O-N-A-C-R-E.
Narrator: Four
Boy: How do you spell your first name?
Girl: C-A-M-I double L-A.
Narrator: Five
Girl: What time does the bus leave this evening?
Boy: Quarter to seven.
Narrator: Six
Boy: How much is the book?
Girl: Three dollars fifty.

Listening Part 4, Exam task Track 7

You will hear a girl, Becky, telling her friend, Milo, about a cookery club. Listen and complete each question.

Becky: Milo, did you know Cookery Club's starting again?

Milo: Really? Is it on Wednesday, like last year?

Becky: No, Friday – Mr Bath told me to tell everyone.

Milo: OK. Are many people doing it this year?

Becky: The new cookery room's got 12 cookers, so Mr Bath says 20 people can join.

Milo: Did he say what we're going to cook this week?

Becky: He's teaching us to make bread. And he'll bring some soup for us to have with it.

Milo: Great!

Becky: Mr Bath won't be here next week, so Miss Donagh will show us how to make something.

Milo: Who? How do you spell her name?

Becky: She's my science teacher. It's D-O-N-A-G-H.

Milo: OK. So is it the same time as last year?

Becky: Yes. School finishes at 3.30, and we all need time to get to the cookery room, so we'll meet at three forty-five, like last year.

Milo: Right. And how much is it?

Becky: It'll be different every week, but not more than £4.50.

Milo: OK. See you there!

Unit 3

Grammar, Exercise 4 Track 8

1 How many apples are there in the bowl?
There are a few apples in the bowl.

2 How much milk is there in the fridge?
There's a little milk in the fridge.

3 How many flowers are there in the garden?
There are a lot of flowers in the garden.

4 How many pictures are there in the hall?
There are a few pictures in the hall.

5 How much meat is there on the plate?
There's a little meat on the plate.

6 How many potatoes are there in the bag?
There are a lot of potatoes in the bag.

7 How much jam is there on the bread?
There's a little jam on the bread.

Vocabulary, Exercise 4 Track 9

1 An omelette is made from eggs.

2 Rice is usually white or brown.

3 People usually make soup with meat or vegetables (or fish).

4 Juice is nice to drink.

5 Salad is usually cold.

6 Chickens are a kind of bird.

7 Fish live in the sea or rivers (and lakes).

8 Onions are round.

Listening Part 5 Track 10

You will hear a woman on the TV talking about a new programme for teenagers. Listen and complete each question.

Sadly, that was the last *Cook it Fast* show, but don't worry, food lovers! There will soon be an exciting new show for teenagers called *Hot Food*. The show will include cooking and information about all kinds of subjects such as healthy food and national dishes. In the first programme, young cooks tell us all about vegetables. They'll show us how to cook and grow them. But this won't be like a normal cookery show: the programmes are not filmed at the TV centre. We're making the programmes in schools! And we'd like you to call us with your ideas – we'll choose the best ones and then come and film you! So phone us on 0996 548013 if you have any brilliant ideas for the programmes. Now get out your diary! This amazing new programme will be on Mondays. And on Tuesday evenings, you'll be able to chat to people from the show online. The first show's on 28th November, after you come home from school, from five fifteen until five forty-five – write it down now!

Unit 4

Vocabulary, Exercise 6 Track 11

1 Do you play volleyball in a team?

2 I'd like to go cycling when we're on holiday.

3 Janey and Maria do aerobics every Monday evening.

4 You must throw the ball over the net.

5 How often do you train for the competition with your coach?

6 I won't be happy if we lose the match.

Listening Part 1 Track 12

You will hear five short conversations. There is one question for each conversation. For each question, choose the right answer (A, B or C).

Narrator: 1 Where is Jessie playing table tennis?

Girl: Where's your sister, Robert?

Boy: Jessie's playing table tennis with her friend, Kate. They went after school.

Girl: To Kate's house, you mean?

Boy: That's right, and they're going to the sports centre to play volleyball after that.

Narrator: 2 What does the girl's football team wear?

Boy: Does your team wear black shirts, like ours?

Girl: With white numbers, yes. Our team wears nearly the same as yours, but our socks are white, not black.

Boy: Oh. So you wear white shorts, too?

Girl: We do, with a black number at the sides.

Narrator: 3 What time is Henry's skiing lesson?

Man: Is your skiing lesson before or after mine, Henry?

Boy: What time's yours, Dad?

Man: 8.45.

Boy:	Oh, well mine starts half an hour later, at quarter past nine. You'll have to get up before me!
Narrator:	4 What is Mum's aerobics teacher doing this evening?
Boy:	Why aren't you at your aerobics class this evening, Mum?
Woman:	Our teacher can't do the class this week.
Boy:	Is she ill again?
Woman:	No, she's fine now. She's flying to Paris tonight because she's got a wedding there tomorrow.
Narrator:	5 Where did Liz sell her football ticket?
Boy:	Liz, hi. Did you sell that football match ticket that you don't want? I just heard someone on the radio asking for tickets.
Girl:	Oh, I've sold mine. I put a poster up at my football club and someone there wanted it.
Boy:	That's good.
Girl:	Yes, Dad advertised it online first, but no one called us about that.

Unit 5

Grammar, Exercise 3 Track 13

Last summer, Simon went with his family to camp in a tent near a castle in the mountains. It was a beautiful place but as soon as they arrived, it started to rain and it didn't stop for four days! During the day, they didn't do any activities because it was too wet outside and at night, they didn't sleep because the wind and the rain were so noisy. On the fifth day, the man who lived in the castle invited them to stay inside the castle! After that, Simon and his family had a great time. They didn't mind the bad weather because they played games in the castle all day and they didn't hear the rain and the wind at night.

Listening Part 5 Track 14

You will hear some information about a museum. Listen and complete each question.

The Museum of Pop Music is the city's most popular museum for visitors aged 12 to 18. And its new address in Victoria Square has brought thousands more visitors to see its amazing collections.

This month, the museum has a new exhibition. It's called 'Cinema' and it explores art and music from film, with hundreds of pictures, recordings and videos. It's open from the 31st October until the 25th November. Don't miss it! The museum has also just opened a new fashion room. Here, you can see a large number of clothes worn by famous pop stars over the last 50 or 60 years.

To make it easier for you to travel to the museum, why don't you come on the boat? Museum visitors can now buy special low-price tickets. It's much nicer than sitting on a bus! Ask about this at any transport office or online.

Museum tickets for adults cost eight pounds fifty, but for children it's just five pounds seventy-five. This includes young people up to the age of 19, but children under five go free.

Unit 6

Grammar, Exercise 4 Track 15

1 Journey C is longer than journey A.
2 Journey A is the shortest.
3 Journey B is further than journey C.
4 Journey A is the longest.
5 Journey B is cheaper than journey A.
6 Journey A is the most expensive.
7 Train B is older than train C.
8 Train C is the newest.

Vocabulary, Exercise 3 Track 16

Narrator:	One
Boy:	How do you usually travel when you go on holiday?
Girl:	We usually travel by train.
Narrator:	Two
Boy:	Do most students walk to your school or do they go by bus or car?
Girl:	Most go by car!
Narrator:	Three
Boy:	Which airport do people in your town fly from?
Girl:	They usually fly from Barcelona airport.
Narrator:	Four
Boy:	Can ten-year-olds drive cars in your country?
Girl:	No, of course they can't!
Narrator:	Five
Boy:	Does anyone in your family ride a motorbike?
Girl:	Yes. My uncle rides one.
Narrator:	Six
Boy:	How long does it take for a ship to sail around the world?
Girl:	I don't know. How long?
Boy:	About three months, I think.

Listening Part 2 Track 17

Listen to Marcia talking to her friend, Josh, about taking the school bus. Where does each person catch the school bus? Write a letter A–H next to each person.

Marcia:	I'm going to start taking the school bus next week, Josh. Where should I catch it?
Josh:	I catch it from Hill Street. After the railway bridge, there's a roundabout and my bus stop's there.
Marcia:	Right. Does Michael catch it there? He lives near you.
Josh:	No. His mum drives him into town. She works at the motorbike shop, but leaves her car in the car park in George Street. Michael catches the bus there.
Marcia:	Right.
Josh:	David gets on at the bus stop in New Street, by the bridge – the one that crosses the river.
Marcia:	Oh yes, I can catch it there too. Who else goes on the bus?

Josh: Ellen. She lives opposite the cinema, so she catches the bus at the tram stop near there.

Marcia: What about Katy, Ellen's neighbour?

Josh: She doesn't like crossing the busy road to the tram stop. So she uses the stop next to the traffic lights behind the station.

Marcia: Oh yes.

Josh: Tom gets the bus too, at the crossing, near the supermarket car park.

Marcia: I know. Thanks Josh ...

Unit 7

Grammar, Exercise 4 Track 18

Girl: Peter is always hungry in the afternoon at school.

Boy: He should eat more at lunchtime.

Girl: Peter often forgets what his homework is.

Boy: He should write it down in a diary or notebook.

Girl: On rainy days, Peter's sweater is always wet.

Boy: He should wear a jacket.

Girl: Peter wants to play tennis better.

Boy: He should take some lessons.

Girl: Peter is always tired in the morning.

Boy: He shouldn't go to bed late.

Girl: Peter's sister is angry with him.

Boy: He shouldn't borrow her things without asking.

Vocabulary, Exercise 3 Track 19

1 Hassan only has lessons at school in the morning.
2 Hassan studies fourteen different subjects at school.
3 A man called Mr Ali teaches Hassan maths.
4 Hassan spends about two hours a night doing his homework.
5 Hassan has only missed one day of school this school year.

Listening Part 5 Track 20

You will hear a music teacher talking about her lessons. Listen and complete each question.

I'm here to tell you about my after-school music lessons at Hill Road School. I'm Mrs Sweet. I know some of you can already play the violin because you learn it in music lessons at school, and I've seen you playing in the school orchestra. But if you'd like to try something else, you can learn to play the guitar with me. I have a class of ten students and we have lots of fun! School orchestra practises on Mondays, and I think it's good for you to have a rest on Tuesdays, so you can come and play more music at my lessons on Wednesdays, starting at four o'clock. We meet for the lessons in Room 58 – that's the big room opposite Art Room seven. If you come, you must buy the book I use so you can practise at home. It's called *Play Well* and you can buy it at Music Now. My lessons aren't expensive because you learn in a group of ten. Each student pays just £22.80 a month, so it's five pounds seventy a week. OK?

Unit 8

Grammar, Exercise 4 Track 21

1 He didn't stop laughing while he was watching the cartoon.
2 She dropped the bowl on her foot while she was putting fruit in it.
3 They saw the circus lorries in the street while they were walking to school.
4 He broke the light on his bike while he was trying to mend the wheel.
5 She was playing a computer game so she didn't hear the phone.
6 We built a fire for the first time while we were camping.

Listening Part 2 Track 22

Listen to Matthew talking to his friend, Alice, about courses his friends took while they were on holiday. Which course did each friend take? For questions 1–5, write a letter A–H next to each friend.

Matthew: How was your holiday, Alice?

Alice: Great. My course was really interesting.

Matthew: What did you learn?

Alice: How to write stories and news articles.

Matthew: Really? Maybe I should do a course on my holiday ...

Alice: Like Ahmet? He learned to cook Chinese dishes on holiday – he wants to work as a food writer when he leaves school.

Matthew: Zena went to the same holiday camp as Ahmet, didn't she?

Alice: Yes, but she chose a course which she didn't need to do lots of reading and writing for. She had a week of Spanish dancing lessons.

Matthew: What about Zena's sister, Leah?

Alice: She learned to work with silver and made a beautiful necklace and earrings. I saw them yesterday.

Matthew: That's amazing. Is Mick on holiday?

Alice: No, he just went away for two days because he had to come home on Monday to do a music exam. He did a windsurfing and sailing course at Lake Jarvis.

Matthew: Right. When does Ellie come home?

Alice: Next week. She's done a short course on biology this week. It was all about water plants and she loved it.

Matthew: Really?

Unit 9

Grammar, Exercise 2 Track 23

1 He's carrying his violin because he's going to play in a concert.
2 He's revising because he's going to do an exam tomorrow.
3 He's waiting in the street because a bus is going to come soon.
4 He's finding his seat in the theatre because the play is going to start soon.
5 He's practising dancing because he's going to a disco later.
6 He needs a knife because he's going to cut the bread.

Listening Part 4 Track 24

You will hear Neil talking to his friend about an art exhibition. Listen and complete each question.

Neil: Maria, do you like this painting?

Maria: It's brilliant, Neil! Did you do it?

Neil: Yes. I'm going to put it in the art club's Young Artists exhibition.

Maria: Great. Will the exhibition only be paintings? Or are there other things as well, like drawings or film?

Neil: There are going to be a few photos in the exhibition, too.

Maria: Really? I must see it. When is it?

Neil: In July, starting on the 24th and finishing on the 30th. Can you come?

Maria: Yes. Where is it?

Neil: At the college. The exhibition entrance is opposite the theatre.

Maria: OK. Are you going to sell the paintings?

Neil: Yes, but quite cheaply. We decided the most expensive price should be £30, but some of the small pictures will cost just £7.50. And we'll give all the money we get to our art club.

Maria: That's good.

Neil: And our teacher is going to give lessons at the exhibition.

Maria: What about?

Neil: She's a really good painter of people. But the subject she's going to teach at the exhibition is colour – so all sorts of artists will be interested.

Unit 10

Grammar, Exercise 3 Track 25

1 She'll go to the lake with Nick if he doesn't have football practice.
2 If she goes to the lake, she'll need her swimming costume.
3 If she takes a picnic, she won't need to buy food in the café.
4 If she cycles around the lake, she'll feel tired.
5 If she sees some interesting animals, she'll take photos of them.
6 She'll put her camera in her bag if it starts to rain.
7 She won't take her rain jacket if the weather is good.

Listening Part 1 Track 26

You will hear five short conversations. There is one question for each conversation. For each question, choose the right answer (A, B or C).

Narrator: 1 What was the weather like last winter?

Man: Look at the snow outside, Daisy!

Daisy: Wow! We can go skiing this weekend – brilliant! We didn't ski last winter at all, did we?

Man: No, it was too wet. But there may be a lot of ice on the roads this weekend, so we may not go skiing.

Daisy: Never mind.

Narrator: 2 Who will go for the birthday meal with Jade and her parents?

Woman: Who's coming to the restaurant with us on your birthday, Jade?

Girl: I asked three of my best friends, Mary, Kate and Emma, but Emma can't come.

Woman: OK, and of course your brother will be with us.

Girl: And you and dad.

Narrator: 3 What happened during the storm last week?

Boy: That storm was terrible last week, wasn't it?

Girl: Yes! A tree fell across the river and the water came up onto the road near our school.

Boy: Was the school OK?

Girl: Yes, but we had to walk there every morning until the water went away.

Narrator: 4 What work does Eleanor do on the farm at weekends?

Boy: Which farm do you work on at weekends, Eleanor?

Girl: The one next to the horse-riding school.

Boy: Cool! They have thousands of chickens – do you have to collect their eggs?

Girl: I do, and my friend Sue sells them in the farm shop.

Narrator: 5 Where is Richard's MP3 player?

Man: Why are you using my MP3 player, Richard?

Richard: Because mine's in Mum's car and she's gone to see Grandma.

Man: Are you sure? I saw it in the kitchen this morning.

Richard: I know, but I went to the library after that. Mum drove me home, and she's just texted me to say she found it on one of the seats.

Unit 11

Grammar, Exercise 3 Track 27

Dad: Hi Adam. What are you doing?

Adam: I've just got home from my music lesson. Have you had dinner yet?

Dad: No, not yet.

Adam: I'm hungry. Do you want me to help you cook?

Dad: No, I've already done it. I prepared the fish this morning and cooked it earlier this evening.

Adam: Great! Let's eat. I'll put the knives and forks on the table.

Dad: I've just done that, a minute ago. But I haven't put any water or glasses on the table yet. Can you do that, please?

Adam: OK.

Listening Part 3 Track 28

Listen to Christina talking to her friend Barney about her health problem. For each question, choose the right answer (A, B or C).

Barney: How are you, Christina?

Christina: Not great.

Barney: What's the matter?

Christina: I've hurt my back, at the top, near my neck. It hurts when I put my arms up.

Barney: Have you seen the doctor?

Christina: Not yet. But I will.

Barney: This morning?

Christina: She's busy – I'm going tomorrow afternoon. So I won't be at school until Thursday.

Barney: How did it happen?

Christina: I fell over after basketball practice yesterday. I walked home from school, then it happened when I was going upstairs to our flat.

Barney: Really? So where are you now?

Christina: At home, lying down. Not on my bed; in the living room, on the sofa. Mum's here, making lunch in the kitchen.

Barney: So what can't you do at the moment?

Christina: Mum said no skateboarding, which I'm not happy about. But I can go swimming – it may help. I'm not going to my guitar lesson this evening, but that's fine!

Barney: Would you like something to read? I've got some new books from the library about famous people.

Christina: OK – but not film actors again.

Barney: A pop singer's life?

Christina: I'd prefer to read about a footballer or something like that.

Barney: How about an amazing swimmer?

Christina: Brilliant. Thanks, Barney.

Unit 12

Grammar, Exercise 3 Track 29

1 The first email was sent in 1971.
2 The first digital cameras were sold by a company called Logitech.
3 The first fridge was built by Jacob Perkins in 1834.
4 The first computer mouse was made of wood.
5 The first hairdryer was used by a French hairdresser.
6 The first text messages were written on the third of December 1992.

Listening Part 2 Track 30

Listen to Alice talking to her mum about finding things on the Internet. What thing does each person want to find? For questions 1–5, write a letter A–H next to each person.

Woman: Hi, Alice.

Girl: Hi, Mum.

Woman: Where's everyone else? Is Aunt Sarah here?

Girl: She's on the computer with Dad. She's looking for a hairdryer that she saw on a TV advertisement.

Woman: What about your dad?

Girl: He wants a DVD. There's a special offer on that one about a photographer – he saw it at the cinema last year.

Woman: Oh, OK. And your brother?

Girl: Thomas is in his bedroom on his phone. He's trying to find a website where he can buy a cheap electric guitar. He wants to teach himself to play guitar.

Woman: Really? And your sister?

Girl: Annabel's on her laptop. She's unhappy because our printer isn't good for photos, so she's looking for a new one.

Woman: Which cousin came with Aunt Sarah?

Girl: John. He's waiting to use the computer so he can look on the Internet. He wants this new digital camera that takes amazing pictures and videos.

Woman: Right. Is Grandma in her room?

Girl: Yes. She's online on her TV. She's asked for a new laptop for her birthday and she's looking at them now.

Woman: Right!

Acknowledgements

Author acknowledgements
The authors and publishers would like to offer many thanks to Emma Heyderman, Anne-Marie Murphy and James Frith for all their input, thanks to Clare Nielsen-Marsh and Judith Greet for their hard work, plus a special thank you to Helena.

Publisher acknowledgements
The authors and publishers are grateful to Joanna Kosta for reviewing the material during the writing process. The publishers would also like to thank Donatella Sancesi (Bologna) and Lisa Foppiani (Genoa) for their help in the early market research stages of the development of this course.

Corpus
Development of this publication has made use of the Cambridge English Corpus (CEC). The CEC is a computer database of contemporary spoken and written English, which currently stands at over one billion words. It includes British English, American English and other varieties of English. It also includes the Cambridge Learner Corpus, developed in collaboration with the University of Cambridge ESOL Examinations. Cambridge University Press has built up the CEC to provide evidence about language use that helps to produce better language teaching materials.

English Profile
This product is informed by the English Vocabulary Profile, built as part of English Profile, a collaborative programme designed to enhance the learning, teaching and assessment of English worldwide. Its main funding partners are Cambridge University Press and Cambridge ESOL and its aim is to create a 'profile' for English linked to the Common European Framework of Reference for Languages (CEF). English Profile outcomes, such as the English Vocabulary Profile, will provide detailed information about the language that learners can be expected to demonstrate at each CEF level, offering a clear benchmark for learners' proficiency. For more information, please visit www.englishprofile.org

Photo acknowledgements
The authors and publishers acknowledge the following sources of copyright material and are grateful for the permissions granted. While every effort has been made, it has not always been possible to identify the sources of all the material used, or to trace all copyright holders. If any omissions are brought to our notice, we will be happy to include the appropriate acknowledgements on reprinting.

The publishers are grateful to the following for permission to reproduce photographic material:

p.7: Alamy/Blend Images; p.11: Alamy/redsnapper; p.14: Corbis/Bloomimage; p.19: Alamy/Steve Morgan; p.22: Alamy/Jeff Greenberg; p.23 (t): Rex Features/Masatoshi Okauchi; p.23 (b): SuperStock/Juice Images; p.24: Getty Images/Tim Stocker Photography/Flickr; p.26: Corbis/ColorBlind Images/Blend Images; p.34: Rex Features; p.36: Corbis/Radius Images; p.38: Alamy/Liz Boyd; p.39:Alamy/flavia raddavero; p.46: Corbis/Yasuo Kondo/Anyone/amanaimages; p.50 (l): Thinkstock/iStockphoto; p.50 (c): Shutterstock/Monkey Business Images; p.50 (r): Shutterstock/Paul Hakimata Photography; p.52: Shutterstock/Iakov Filimonov; p.55: SuperStock/LumiImages/Mauritius; p.56 (t): Alamy/David Rowland; p.56 (b): Alamy/Gary Dyson.

Cover photos:
(t): Shutterstock/Zurijeta; (cl): Shutterstock/ Pressmaster; (c): Shutterstock/AVAVA; (cr): Shutterstock/Zurijeta; (b): Shutterstock/michaeljung.

Picture research by Louise Edgeworth

Text acknowledgements
The authors and publishers acknowledge the following sources of copyright material and are grateful for the permissions granted. While every effort has been made, it has not always been possible to identify the sources of all the material used, or to trace all copyright holders. If any omissions are brought to our notice, we will be happy to include the appropriate acknowledgements on reprinting.

Telegraph Media Group Limited for the text on p. 34 adapted from 'Katie Melua's holiday heaven and hell' by Caroline Shearing, The Telegraph, 22.10.12. Copyright © Telegraph Media Group Limited 2012.

Illustrations by:
David Benham (GCI Illustration) pp 4, 16, 32; John Batten (Beehive Illustration) pp. 5(t), 9, 10, 18, 29, 42, 47, 52, 57; Kate Rochester (Pickled Ink) pp. 5(b), 12, 13, 17, 25, 30, 45, 48, 55; Richard Jones (Beehive Illustration) pp. 6, 20, 40, 41, 44; Simon Smith (Beehive Illustration) pp. 21, 28, 33, 53, 54;

Design, layout and art edited by: Wild Apple Design Ltd.